SIR
ROBERT
PEEL

SIR ROBERT PEEL

JUSTIN McCARTHY

NONSUCH

First published 1891
Copyright © in this edition Nonsuch Publishing, 2007

Nonsuch Publishing
Cirencester Road, Chalford, Stroud, Gloucestershire, GL6 8PE
www.nonsuch-publishing.com

Nonsuch Publishing is an imprint of NPI Media Group

British Library Cataloguing in Publication Data.
A catalogue record for this book is available from the British Library.

ISBN 978 1 84588 601 1

Typesetting and origination by NPI Media Group
Printed in Great Britain

Contents

Introduction to the
Modern Edition

S IR ROBERT PEEL (1788–1850) was twice Prime Minister of Britain. His period spent in government, as premier and in other offices, saw a series of landmark social reforms that radically altered society at the time. Legislation was pushed through that cut working hours for women and children and created cheap and regular rail services. His creation of the Metropolitan Police in 1829 completely reorganised the way London was policed, something he achieved despite powerful opposition, and would form the basis of the modern police force. The repeal of the Corn Laws, perhaps his most famous action, caused splits within his party, who refused to support a policy so unpopular with landowners; but the humanitarian nature of his actions afforded him lasting popularity with ordinary people. It did, however, drive his own party into the political wilderness of futile opposition during the years following his resignation, something which makes Peel a controversial figure—at least amongst Conservatives.

Robert Peel was born on 5 February 1788 at Chamber Hall near Bury in Lancashire. He was the eldest son of eleven children born to Robert Peel and Ellen Yates. The Peel family originated in Yorkshire and later moved to Lancashire, where they were weavers and farmers, before progressing into textile manufacture and making their fortune. In the 1790s Robert Peel senior migrated south to Staffordshire. His calico-printing business had made him one of the richest industrialists in Britain: he was able to acquire Drayton Manor and achieve the rank and consequence in society that he had been hoping for, first entering Parliament as the Member for Tamworth in 1790 and then being created a baronet in 1800. He had great ambitions for his eldest son, whom he had educated at home before sending him first to Harrow School and then to Christ Church College, Oxford. The young Robert Peel certainly lived up to his father's expectations: he achieved a double First in Classics and Mathematics & Physics in 1804 and was awarded his M.A. in 1814. His father then focused on grooming him for a career in politics, buying him his first Commons seat in 1809, in Cashel, Tipperary. Peel, at twenty-one, made his maiden speech on 23 January 1810, and was rewarded with applause for his efforts. It was famously described by the Speaker of the House of Commons as 'the best first speech since that of William Pitt'. This was to be the start of a long parliamentary career that was to last until his death in 1850.

Like his father before him, Robert Peel entered the House of Commons in support of the Duke of Portland's Tory government. He made an immediate impact and was, in 1810, appointed as Under-Secretary for War and the Colonies in Spencer Perceval's ministry. He worked with, and was influenced by, Lord Liverpool, as well as other key members of the cabinet, Lords Sidmouth and Castlereagh. Following the assassination of Perceval, Liverpool formed a new ministry and Peel was appointed to one of the most difficult offices in government—that of Chief Secretary for Ireland. His many duties included maintaining order in Ireland, administering the patronage of Ireland on behalf of the British government and preserving the Protestant ascendancy, all of which were undertaken by Peel with a characteristic determination. He wished to rule in Ireland by existing laws, though was forced to institute new measures such as the peace preservation force (which later became the Royal Irish Constabulary) in response to disorders in June 1814. He tried to eradicate corruption within the Irish government by opposing the practices of selling public offices and dismissing civil servants for political action. It is, however, for his strong opposition to Catholic Emancipation that Peel is often remembered in this role.

His attempt to suppress the Catholic Board, an organisation started by Daniel O'Connell, marked the beginning of a long conflict between the two men, earning Robert Peel the nickname 'Orange Peel' and leading to an abortive duel which was prevented only because O'Connell was arrested en route to it. Peel cemented his reputation for being virulently opposed to Catholic Emancipation when he spoke in a House of Commons debate in 1817, and, as a result, he also won the parliamentary seat for Oxford University, who praised him for his 'services to Protestantism'. Peel was by this time exhausted by his position in Ireland, which required frequent travel to London and back, and he resigned the post in 1818, spending the next four years out of office. During this time he married Julia Floyd and the couple had five sons and two daughters.

In 1822 Peel rejoined Lord Liverpool's government as Home Secretary. The next five years saw a large-scale reform of the legal system, with Peel looking intently at flaws within the criminal law and successfully repealing (either partially or wholly) more than 250 outdated statutes as a result—particularly those offences which still carried the death penalty. Canning described Peel as 'the most efficient home secretary that this country ever saw', an impressive accolade considering Peel was only thirty-four when he took up the post. Peel next began to look into the state of the policing of the capital. He proposed that a House of Commons Select Committee should be set up under his chairmanship; this was accepted, but the report concluded that an effective system of policing could not be reconciled with a free society. Many people at this time saw the repressiveness of continental police regimes and believed a similar system in Britain would be a threat to civil liberty. However, the current system was clearly failing, as crime was on the rise despite the catalogue of harsh punishments meted out by the old watch system. Peel's successive attempts continued to meet with opposition until a select committee finally agreed to back him in 1829, and he drew up a bill establishing a new 'Metropolitan Police Force,' with the first 'Bobbies' (a nickname they owed to Peel himself) going out on the beat two months later.

During this time Robert Peel had spent a period out of office (while Canning was Prime Minister) but had returned to his post of Home Secretary under the Duke of Wellington in 1828. It was at this time that Peel's stance against Catholic Emancipation collapsed, as he acknowledged that the growing threat of civil strife in Ireland was greater than that of emancipation. He faced harsh criticism for his changed opinions, though he defended it by quoting William Pitt in saying 'to maintain a consistent attitude amid changed circumstances is to be a slave of the most idle vanity'.

In 1830 Wellington's government was replaced by a ministry headed by Earl Grey. Peel was now, for the first time, a member of the Opposition, as well as M.P. for the family borough of Tamworth, following his father's death. The Tories had by this time split into the Ultras and the Moderates: the latter group called themselves 'conservatives,' willing to contemplate reform but intent on conserving what they saw as the best of society. From this point until 1841 Peel did not hold office, apart from the 'Hundred Days' he spent as Prime Minister in 1834, when he immediately called a general election and issued what became known as the Tamworth Manifesto. In this he pledged his acceptance of the 1832 Reform Act (which he had previously opposed) and argued for a policy of moderate reforms that would preserve important traditions. This marked a shift from the old repressive Toryism to a more enlightened Conservatism, something not to be welcomed by more traditional Tories. Peel, however, did gain more supporters, but there were still more Whigs than Tories in the House of Commons and by 1835 he was tired of being constantly outvoted, and decided to resign. It was not until 1841 that Peel was again asked to become Prime Minister under a Conservative government. This second ministry saw a range of economic reforms including a series of Railway Acts, the Mines Act of 1842 and the Factory Act of 1844. The defining challenge of Peel's career came when he attempted to repeal the Corn Laws in order to alleviate the suffering in Ireland where the Potato Famine was raging. He faced resistance from landowners and a lack of support from his own party, and the repeal was only pushed through months later with the support of the Whigs and the Radicals. Peel resigned on the same day, and never held office again, while his party remained in opposition for the next two decades as a result of his actions. Peel nevertheless continued to attend the House of Commons and gave support to Lord John Russell and his administration in 1846–1847. On 28 June 1850 he gave an important speech on Greece and the foreign policy of Lord Palmerston; the following day he fell from his horse while riding up Constitution Hill, and died just days later.

Modern views of Robert Peel are mixed. While he is certainly credited for the vast changes he made during his two ministries, and often hailed as the father of the modern Conservative party, he is also frequently damned for his apparent betrayal of the party on more than one occasion—his support of Catholic Emancipation (after years of opposition) and the repeal of the Corn Laws in particular. The economic liberalism of the latter move, which was entirely at odds with traditional Tory principles, was bound to result in party division. It is nevertheless clear that Peel had a great impact upon society with his modest reforms, many of which—the modern police force to name but one—have lasted to this day.

I

Peel's Family and Early Career

Peele Fold—The Peeles and Peels—The first Sir Robert Peel—Birth of the great Robert Peel—His Harrow days—His schoolfellows—Lord Byron—His training for Parliament—He becomes member for Cashel—His early success in debate

SIR ROBERT PEEL STANDS HIGH in the line of succession to Robert Walpole; that line of succession in which William the younger stood, and in which Mr Gladstone now stands. These men have nothing to do with the statesmanship which comes in the line of succession to Bolingbroke. A statesman of the Walpole line must be a sound financier; he must be always in earnest, and he must concern himself more readily and naturally with domestic interests than with foreign affairs. Some English politicians of great ability and great patriotic sincerity have always held that the business of English statesmanship was, properly, more in foreign affairs than in domestic work, seeing that England has dominions scattered over all parts of the world.

One of our modern Prime Ministers—Lord Beaconsfield—argued gravely that England must be regarded as an Oriental power. It is not necessary to discuss any of these questions now. The fact has only to be noted that a statesman of such opinions, whether they be right or wrong, could not belong to what may be called the Walpole order, and that to the Walpole order Sir Robert Peel distinctly belongs.

Sir Robert Peel was born near Bury, in Lancashire, on February 5, 1788. He came into the world just after the triumphant American colonists had finally adopted the Constitution of the United States; just before the outbreak of the French Revolution. He came of a family of English yeomanry 'the members of which have been described as happy in a golden mean—too high for the office of constable, and too low for that of sheriff.' These words are quoted from the interesting *Sketch of the Life and Character of Sir Robert Peel*, published in 1860 by his cousin, Sir Lawrence Peel. This book is described by its author as written by one 'near in blood to the deceased; but not too near, as he trusts, for impartiality.' It seems to be written in a spirit of thorough impartiality, and here and there in a temper of almost severe criticism. The family history of the elder generations of the Peels—and, indeed, of all the generations down to Peel's own time—appears exactly what one might have expected for the purpose of bringing forth just such a man. Anyone familiar with the career and the personal character of Sir Robert Peel, but ignorant— if we can suppose such a person possible—of all the story of his ancestors, might easily have constructed for himself a description of the Peels of the past from a study of their greatest descendant. Simplicity, energy, patience, a constant struggle between humour and shyness, a tendency to bashful silence, with, at the same time, great power of speech, an utter absence of all affectation or ostentation—such were the family characteristics which were glorified in the career and the personal peculiarities of Sir Robert Peel. There was thus, as his relative says, 'a mixture in his origin and fortunes of two conditions of life—a Tory and a democrat.'

The history of the Peel family is traced back to Craven, in Yorkshire, in the year 1600, there or thereabouts; but not very long afterwards they removed to the neighbourhood of Blackburn, in Lancashire. The family name was spelled Peele during many generations. There was a Robert Peel, a manufac- turer of woollen cloth, in Blackburn, about 1640, who is said to have been the first really prosperous man of the family. One of his sons, Robert —the name of Robert is everywhere in the Peel family—bought a small estate near Blackburn, to which he gave the name of Peele Fold, and which still bears the name, and is in the possession of the family. His son, William, was the father of another Robert Peele, who was the grandfather of the great Prime Minister. This Robert Peele dropped the final letter of the name which the family were then bearing, for the very characteristic reason that it was a waste of a letter, as the 'e' affected in no wise the sound of the word. He, and a brother-in-law, and one or two other partners, formed a company, and set up a calico-printing factory, and established a warehouse in Manchester. His sons, we read, were, like himself, hard-working, industrious, plain, frugal, reserved, and shy; 'nourishing,' says Sir Lawrence Peel, 'a sort of defensive pride.' The expression, defensive pride, is very happy. Sir Lawrence Peel, per- haps, did not remember that Samuel Johnson used it once on a memorable occasion. He and some of his friends were talking over the story of his quarrel with Lord Chesterfield. Johnson declared that Chesterfield was the proudest man then existing. Someone said, 'I think, from your own account, you were the prouder man of the two.' 'But mine,' replied Johnson, instantly, 'was defensive pride.' The listeners thought this a very happy description and justification of his feeling. So it was. The phrase is also used very happily in regard to the Peels. The pride of Sir Robert Peel was altogether a defensive pride. It never had anything aggressive in it. It was the defensive pride of a shy and sensitive man, conscious of his weakness.

Of Robert Peel, the economist of letters, another Robert, the first baronet of the family, and the father of the Prime Minister, was the son. This Robert Peel followed the ways of his father and his other relatives in sticking close to his business, and paying strict attention to all new developments in mechanism and industrial art which had any bearing on its operation. He did not invent any improvements of his own, but he took early advantage of every fresh and genuine discovery or application; and he made a great fortune, and went into Parliament. He sat in the House of Commons for several years as a Tory, and he was by no means an undistinguished member of the House. He made a speech, in 1799, in favour of the Union of Great Britain and Ireland, which seems to have created some impression. He sat for the borough of Tamworth during seven successive Parliaments, and gave a constant support to the Tory leaders. In 1800 he was made a baronet, and he remained in the House of Commons until 1820. Then he fell back into private life. He lived for ten years—lived to see the rise of his son's renown. In the coming of that renown he had long believed. The story of Sir Robert Peel, the statesman, is one of those rarest of all in real life,—the story of a young man elected to greatness in anticipation by his family, and afterwards actually ratifying the election by his career. The elder Robert Peel determined that no effort should be spared to educate his son up to the level of the career to which he believed him destined. Young Robert himself was a studious boy, anxious to cultivate his own mind and his own faculties to their very utmost; rather inclined, perhaps, to over-cultivation. He was sent to Harrow, where he became a schoolfellow of Lord Byron. Byron wrote of him long after: 'Peel, the orator and statesman—that was, or is, or is to be—was my form-fellow, and we were both at the top of our remove. We were on good terms; but his brother was my intimate friend. There were always great hopes of Peel amongst us all, masters and scholars, and he has not disappointed them. As a scholar, he was greatly my superior; as a declaimer and actor, I was reckoned at least his equal; as a schoolboy, out of school, I was always in scrapes, and he never; and in school he always knew his lesson, and I rarely; but when I knew it well, I knew it nearly as well; and in general information, history, &c., I think I was

his superior.' Byron's comparison or contrast of himself and Peel seems to be
candid and fair. It is a curious fact, however, that Byron rates himself above
Peel as a declaimer, and that Peel turned out to be one of the most perfect
masters of the art of Parliamentary declamation, while Byron failed as an orator in the House of Lords, mainly because it was thought that his declamation
was stilted, artificial, and of the school of the suburban melodrama. It has to
be observed that Peel began with the priceless possession of a noble voice,
sweet, strong, capable of the freest expansion. Byron was Peel's senior only by
a few days. Byron left Harrow in 1805, and the two schoolfellows went their
widely different ways. Each remained, however, at the top of his own remove.
Byron walked, as Carlyle says of Danton, 'his own wild road, whither that led
him.' Peel moved steadily, patiently, soberly along his road, which certainly
was not wild, and it led him to a lofty place.

Peel continued to be a shy and studious youth. So shy was he, that in his
walks he would sometimes make a long circuit to avoid the meeting with
noisy and demonstrative groups of village boys. After he had left Harrow
he went to Oxford, and studied hard there, and took his BA degree there in
1808; and by that time he was nearly qualified in years to enter the House
of Commons. It was easy for a man of influence and great wealth like the
elder Peel, who had long been a devoted follower of the Tory leaders, to
find a constituency for his son. A seat was found for Peel in the Irish city
of Cashel—the city, now a decayed little town, nestling at the foot of a
ruin-crowned rock which can be seen with deep interest and delight even
by a traveller who has lately stood on the Acropolis at Athens. Peel, then,
entered the House of Commons as member for an Irish constituency. He
came into the House of Commons in 1809, the year in which Byron took
his seat for the first time in the House of Lords.

Peel followed the conventional way of the period, and did not address
the House of Commons during his first session. At that time, and for long
after, it was thought rather presumptuous and unbecoming for a very young
member to take any part in debate. It was held to be at once modest and
cautious to make one's self well acquainted with all the ways of the House;
to get to understand its feelings as well as its rules; to become acclimatised
to its atmosphere before attempting to address Mr Speaker. For one session at least it was recommended that young members should refrain from
taking part in discussion. Some wise veterans of the House of Commons
even went so far as to recommend three sessions of silent observation. A
young member was supposed to keep on gradually qualifying himself for
a speech by becoming bolder and more emphatic in his occasional cries of

'hear, hear,' and 'order, order.' Thus he grew accustomed to the sound of his own voice, and no longer shrank back into his seat utterly abashed if, having ventured on a rash 'hear, hear,' he found that his was the sole sound of approval heard in the House. In our days we have changed all that. It is by no means an uncommon thing for a new member to speak the very first day of his Parliamentary career. Nobody, now, who believes he can speak—and most men have this belief about themselves—would think of sitting in silence during a whole session. The man who remains silent for his first session now is, probably, a man who hopes to be allowed to remain silent for his second, third, and fourth session—for all his sessions.

The reason for this change in Parliamentary ways is not to be found altogether in an increasing lack of reverence for the House of Commons, or an increasing amount of self-conceit in the young members of the present day. The truth is, that not many constituencies in our time would like their representative to sit silent during the whole of his first session. The people of Cashel, when Peel represented it, did not care whether the member for Cashel ever opened his mouth in the House. He did not represent the people of Cashel. He had nothing to do with them, nor they with him. The local magnate elected him, or appointed him, and that was all. The public in general took but little interest in the speeches that were made in Parliament; there were no cheap newspapers to bring the account of what had been done in Westminster under the eyes of the very poorest householder in the land. The condition of things is now quite different. The people are represented; the constituencies are really constituencies. Every constituent wants to know what sort of a figure his representative is making in the House, and how he is acting with regard to this or that political or social controversy. Constituencies now, as a rule, do not like silent members. A man must be very popular in his constituency, or have rendered some signal service in public, to be allowed to indulge, without remonstrance, in a luxury of discreet silence. That sense of quickened interest among the constituencies in what their representatives are doing is anything but an unhealthy sign of the times, or a thing to be deprecated. It is a very healthy sign. It is a thing, on the whole, to be glad of. But, like other good things, it is not an unqualified blessing, and it brings with it the disadvantage —for a disadvantage, on the whole, it is—that a member of Parliament can hardly wait now to study the ways and master the forms of the House of Commons before rising to address the Speaker.

Peel remained silent, then, during the whole of his first session. When Parliament reassembled, in January 1810, he had the honour of seconding the Address in reply to the Speech from the Throne. Then he made his maiden speech. 'A little cold,' Guizot declared the maiden speech to be. In the House of Commons it would seem, however, to have been regarded as a distinct success. The voice of the young orator and his whole mode of delivery were decidedly in his favour. The House of Commons always welcomes with fresh delight any one who has a fine voice and a clear delivery. A man thus endowed starts in the House with as much in his favour as a man who starts in the world with a fortune. The man with the voice may prove to be voice and nothing else; the man with a fortune may prove to have only the gift of muddling the fortune away. But in either case the advantage is there to begin with. Peel's voice and manner secured him attention, and even admiration. As to the matter of the speech, there was not, and really could not have been, much in it. The man who moves the Address has very little chance of being able to say anything new; the man who seconds it has no chance at all. One added difficulty was put in Peel's way. It was the wish and the policy of the Government, or, at least, of the Prime Minister, that the Address itself, and the speeches delivered in proposing and seconding it, should convey as little as possible to the mind of Parliament and the public. The Minister was waiting for a policy; waiting for a wind. So much the more credit, therefore, is due to Peel's maiden speech in the fact that, despite these hampering and harassing conditions, it did seize and hold the attention of the House, and did make members in general believe that they were listening to something which was worth the hearing.

Peel was tall, and at this early period of his career well formed. He was slender, and there was what certain modern writers would probably call a 'willowy' gracefulness about him. He had good features, a well-formed head, with a large forehead—at that time regarded as an indispensable attribute of intellect—and a singularly sweet smile. He was then what would be called a dressy man. People still used to powder their hair, and the powder, it is said, became Peel very well. A little later on O'Connell scoffed at him as 'a young man not past the foppery of perfumed handkerchiefs and thin shoes.' He was of very active habits, and much given to athletic sports. He was a good walker, was fond of shooting, and was a good shot. He had an immense amount of humour in him, to which he allowed all too rare an expression. He had a keen sense of the ridiculous which, however, he only permitted to expand when he was in the company of his closest friends. He appears to have lived in a constant struggle between his keen sense of the ridiculous and his somewhat overwrought and morbid notions as to propriety and decorum. Those who knew him only from the outside thought him merely a cold, stiff, proud young man, pedantically given up to the conventionalities and the proprieties. He was not proud, but only shy; he was not stiff but only reserved and habitually silent. He enjoyed wit and humour far more than most men do, even among those who are in no wise restrained by the conventionalities and the proprieties.

He was well-versed in literature, classical and modern. His classic reading did not pretend to be scholarship even then, and certainly would not be considered scholarship now; but he was unquestionably a very well-read man in the classics, and would be considered so even in our days. He had a genuine relish for art of every kind. He had a singularly happy gift of quotation. Later on, he was accused by Mr Disraeli of never using a quotation the success of which with the House of Commons was not already guaranteed by its often having been successful there before. But Mr Disraeli did not much care at that time what he said about an opponent so long as he disparaged him. No man ever indulged less in hackneyed quotations than Peel; and he had very often a peculiarly felicitous freshness in the manner in which he brightened a debate by some appropriate citation. He had studied closely and worked hard for the business of debate. His father was in the habit of taking him to the House of Commons to hear the discussions. Peel had listened to Fox and to Pitt; he had heard the last utterances of that splendid school of Parliamentary orators whose triumphs are but a tradition to us. It is a proof of that originality of mind which his opponents were accustomed to deny to him, that he did not allow his eloquence to be formed on the model of a school which was passing away. The House of Commons was becoming every year more and more an assembly of businessmen. The eloquence which in the future would command that House must have a good deal of business-precision and practicality about it. The House of Commons of later days—even of Peel's earliest days—would, probably, not listen to speeches in such a style of eloquence as those of the elder, or even the younger, Pitt. It is a well-known and well-authenticated Parliamentary anecdote, that when Canning ventured on his famous antithesis about calling in the New World to redress the balance of the Old, it was a mere case of touch and go whether the House would break into applause or burst into laughter. Canning's courage was rewarded; the House broke into applause, and posterity has consented to echo the plaudits every now and then. But Peel understood the growing change in the taste and temper of the House of Commons, and he adapted his eloquence to the new conditions. It is hard to say whether we have gained or lost by the gradual disuse of the higher forms of eloquence in Parliament. The speeches are as long now as speeches ever were, and in the House of Commons there are not half a dozen really eloquent men.

The first really eloquent speech which Peel delivered in the House of Commons was a panegyric on Wellington, whom, curiously enough, he had never seen up to that time, and did not see for a long time after. The whole character of Wellington as a soldier and a man was calculated to impress a nature like Peel's most profoundly. But the fairness and the logic of Peel's mind were shown by the fact that, at a time when almost everyone in England was furiously denouncing Napoleon Bonaparte, and trying to make him out an incapable pretender, and even a coward, Peel more than once, in private, broke into an impassioned panegyric of Napoleon's genius as a soldier and a statesman. He deplored what he justly considered as the low moral nature of the great conqueror, but he could not restrain himself from almost unqualified admiration of his genius, both in war and government. It may seem but poor praise to a public man to show that he could be candid enough to admit genius in an enemy of his country; one must see genius, it may he said, as one must see the sun, unless he be blind. But those who will read anything of English journalism and English gossip about the time when Napoleon's career was drawing to its close, will do justice to Peel's clearness and candour. It was an article of faith with most Englishmen then, that Napoleon was not merely a monster of wickedness, and of deliberate wickedness, but that he was a military impostor, a ruler of the order of *Bombastes Furioso*, a liar, a glutton, a bully, and a coward.

II

In Office

The Perceval ministry—Peel Under-Secretary for the Colonies— Perceval killed—Lord Liverpool Prime Minister—Peel Chief Secretary to the Lord Lieutenant—The Catholic question—Peel's quarrel with O'Connell

WHEN PEEL ENTERED PARLIAMENT THE long struggle against Napoleon was still going on—had not, indeed, reached its highest pitch of intensity. The fortunes of England were not as yet showing very brightly. The year 1809 was the period of Corunna, of the disastrous Walcheren Expedition, and of the charges of maladministration in the Army brought against the Duke of York. There was much discontent in many parts of England; there were loud demands for Parliamentary reform, and meetings were held, which here and there ended in riots. The Catholic question was making itself heard. The short lucid interval enjoyed by the poor old King, George III, was soon about to come to a close, never to return. The tendencies in political life—that is, among the men who were qualified to lead political life—were towards electoral reform, towards Catholic Emancipation, and towards Free Trade, this latter tendency showing itself only in a groping sort of way. The foremost statesman of the day, Canning, was now in favour of Catholic Emancipation, and, indeed, had probably been always, at heart, in favour of it. He was moving decidedly in the direction of Free Trade. He was not in favour of Parliamentary reform, or of a general removal of religious disability; but his was a mind that could move quickly towards the right end. The extreme of Toryism was represented by Lord Eldon, a man for whom at first Peel felt a very strong admiration. Lord Liverpool was only a shade less deeply dyed in old-fashioned Toryism than Lord Eldon. Of Peel himself, Guizot says that he was born a Tory.

So he was, if we do not take the saying too literally. But he was also born an intellectual creature, and it was the peculiar characteristic of his mind as he grew up that he must always take account of realities. He very soon began to find his sympathies drawn more and more away from Lord Eldon and towards Mr Canning. By tradition, by teaching, by the conditions of his family, by his bringing-up, and by deep religious feelings, he was made at first a resolute opponent of the demand for Catholic Emancipation. He believed that it would be morally wrong to admit the Catholics to religious equality with those who professed the doctrines of the State Church established by law. He did not believe it would be possible to admit the Catholics of Ireland to religious equality and still maintain the Irish Established Church, or even the Act of Union itself. On the State Church question time has proved that Peel was right. When the Irish Catholics were allowed to vote, the Irish State Church was foredoomed. When the great majority of the people were enfranchised, there could be no hope that the Church of a very small minority would be allowed to remain endowed and established. Most persons now would, very properly, say that this fact, even if generally anticipated, ought to have been only one other reason for emancipating the Catholics. The State Church in England, whatever may be thought of the principle of establishment, rests on a foundation totally unlike that of the Irish State Church. The two institutions represented diametrically opposite principles. The English Church claimed to be the State Church because it was the Church within whose fold the great majority of the English people was sheltered; the Irish Church could only rest its claims on the right of conquest. The vast majority of the people whose Church it professed to be could not be induced by any penal threats or terrors to cross, even once, its threshold. It is necessary to bear these facts in mind in order that we may be able afterwards to understand the meaning of Peel's change of action on the great question of Catholic Emancipation.

The Duke of Portland was at the head of the Government when Peel came into the House of Commons. The Duke of Portland was an amiable and upright man, of only moderate ability. He had been trained by long practice into the business-work of routine statesmanship, and in the House of Lords he made as good a figure for a Ministry as another. He had been for a short time at the head of the famous Coalition Ministry, of which Fox was the soul and the brain. He had acted with the Whigs until, like Burke, he took fright at the early excesses of the French Revolution. Canning was Foreign Secretary; Perceval lent his mediocre intelligence to the business of Chancellor of the Exchequer; Lord Hawkesbury, afterwards Earl of Liverpool, was Home Secretary; Huskisson, a man of genuine capacity and promise, was Secretary to the Treasury; Lord Castlereagh, Secretary for War and the Colonies; and Eldon was Lord Chancellor. Peel's first connection with office of any kind was when he became private secretary to Lord Liverpool. The leading men in the House of Commons at that time, and for some time to come, were Canning and Lord Castlereagh on the Ministerial benches; and among the Whigs, Sheridan still kept up the associations of the most brilliant days of the party, and Brougham had just begun to flash upon the House the eccentric light of his rhetorical genius. Tierney was there, and Romilly and Homer, and the solid, cool, clear headed Samuel Whitbread, and the by no means solid or very clear-headed Sir Francis Burdett. At this stage of his career Burdett was one of the most extreme of Radicals. He was member for Westminster, and had for his colleague another wild and extreme Radical, Lord Cochrane, afterwards Earl of Dundonald, the daring and brilliant seaman, one of the very last of the brave race of the sea-Kings of England. Cochrane was an ardent, a sincere, and a consistent Radical. About this time, however, his energy was employed for the most part in a different occupation from that of politics: he was harassing Napoleon's admirals on the seas; he was destroying the French men-of-war in the Basque Roads. The business of war, in which Cochrane took so active a part, interfered much with the progress of domestic reforms in Parliament, and left to young men like Robert Peel but little chance of distinguishing themselves much in debate.

The Duke of Portland resigned office in 1809, and was succeeded by Mr Spencer Perceval, a man of respectable character and very meagre abilities—perhaps one of the least gifted of English Prime Ministers. Why he ever should have been Prime Minister is still a wonder and a puzzle, even if we make full allowance for the unwillingness of the King to see the highest place in the Government given to Canning. Canning himself had resigned office in consequence of his duel with Lord Castlereagh, which sprang out of their quarrels and recriminations over the unfortunate Walcheren Expedition; and he did not come back under Perceval. In the Perceval Administration, Perceval became First Lord of the Treasury, and also Chancellor of the Exchequer. The Marquis of Wellesley was, for a time, Foreign Secretary; Lord Liverpool was Secretary for the Colonies and War; Lord Eldon remained Lord Chancellor.

Perhaps the two appointments which now interest us most in this Administration of Spencer Perceval's are that of the Secretary at War—a quite different office from that of Secretary for War and the Colonies—and that of the Under Secretary of State for the Colonies. The new Secretary at War was Lord Palmerston; the new Under-Secretary for the Colonies was Robert Peel.

The Perceval Administration was suddenly brought to an end by the act of a madman—at least, of a man who had allowed a supposed grievance to brood upon his mind until it goaded him into insanity. This was a man named Bellingham, who had been for some time a resident in Russia, and conceived himself to have some claims against the Russian Government, which he appealed to the English Government to take up. Nothing came of his appeal; in all probability, nothing could have come of it. Bellingham fed upon the poison of his supposed grievance until his perverted reason could be satisfied with no other resolve than that of killing the first member of the Government who came within his reach. In the lobby of the House of Commons he one day saw the Prime Minister, and although, as he after-wards frankly acknowledged, he had no particular wish to kill Mr Perceval, yet, as Mr Perceval happened to be there, he thought he was bound by his vow to kill him. He fired at him, accordingly, with a pistol, and Perceval fell dead. Bellingham was found guilty—indeed, no finding was needed, for he openly avowed the deed—and although most people regarded him as a mere madman, he was executed in the ordinary course of criminal law. He had done something for Spencer Perceval. Perceval, who would otherwise have hardly been remembered at all, or, if remembered, would have been borne in memory only as the butt of some of Sydney Smith's jokes, was by the bullet of the murderer's pistol exalted to the apotheosis of heroism and martyrdom.

On the death of Perceval, Lord Liverpool became Prime Minister; Lord Eldon continued to be Lord Chancellor; Lord Palmerston remained Secretary at War. Lord Castlereagh, who had become Foreign Secretary during the later period of the Perceval Administration, continued to be Foreign Secretary still. Lord Sidmouth, the Addington of whom it once was epigrammatically said that Pitt was to him as London is to Paddington, and whose descent from the Speaker's chair in order to ascend to the place of Prime Minister was made the occasion for some of Sheridan's most brilliant and telling strokes of Parliamentary sarcasm and wit—Lord Sidmouth became Home Secretary. Most of the other appointments do not greatly concern us. The one appoint-ment which does concern us is that of Chief Secretary to the Lord Lieutenant of Ireland. This office, it may be remarked, is very commonly, but very inac-curately, described as that of the Secretary for Ireland. There is, of course, no Secretary for Ireland. The office is that of Chief Secretary to the Lord Lieutenant of Ireland; and in the Administration of Lord Liverpool this office was given, in the first instance, to Sir Robert Peel.

Never, probably, was a young and gifted statesman put in a position of greater difficulty. Indeed, difficulty is not the word to express adequately the hopeless nature of the position in which Peel was placed. The office was an impossibility, so far as success was concerned. Had Peel been Carteret, Chesterfield, and Fitzwilliam all in one, he could not have made much of the office of Chief Secretary to the Lord Lieutenant in such a juncture of affairs. Ireland was torn by two passionate agitations, one inspired by popular hatred of the Act of Union, the other by the demand of the Irish Catholics for emancipation from the degrading disqualifications placed upon them by law. The Act of Union had hardly been passed when the rebellion of Robert Emmet broke out, as a protest against the extinction of the Irish Parliament. The rebellion was easily put down—it never had a ghost of a chance—and Robert Emmet was executed. But his death had only given new life to the popular feeling, and Emmet was, and still is, a young hero and martyr in the eyes of the vast majority of his countrymen. The Catholic movement had assumed tremendous proportions. It was now under the guidance and inspiration of a man of genius, a master-spirit. Daniel O'Connell had become the leader of the Irish people. He was a Catholic lawyer of good family; he was a most brilliant and successful advocate at the Irish bar; he was, probably, one of the greatest popular orators the world of agitation has ever known, He was a man of lofty stature and of commanding presence, and he had a voice which, for strength, resonance, flexibility, and music, could hardly ever have been surpassed. He had a marvellous combination of daring and of craft. His training as a lawyer enabled him to know exactly what to say in order to arouse his countrymen, and what to leave unsaid in order not to arouse to any purpose the Irish law officers of Dublin Castle. It may be said at once of O'Connell now—of a man denounced in his own day as man was hardly ever denounced, accused of selfishness, lying, cowardice, and all manner of basenesses—it may be said of him now, without fear of contradiction or even cavil, that he was an unselfish man, a wise reformer, and a sincere patriot. The writer of this volume once asked Mr Gladstone what he, who well remembered O'Connell, regarded as O'Connell's chief characteristic. Mr Gladstone thought for a moment, and then said that, in his opinion, the principal characteristic of O'Connell was 'a passion of philanthropy.' The expression was a superb one, regarded merely as a phrase, and it seems to have been applied with justice. O'Connell, during all his career, was devotedly on the side of every measure that tended to the benefit of the poor and the oppressed. He was an impassioned advocate of the abolition of slavery; he was a Free-trader; he was on the side of religious equality; he lent his influence to the mitigation of prison discipline and of the criminal code. The great English philanthropic reformers found that they could count on his steady, earnest support in every one of the measures they had at heart, even though they were unable to give any support to the movement which he had mainly at heart. At this period, however, he was at the head of the Catholic

Association, an organisation formed to advocate the claims of the Catholics to political freedom, and the Catholic question was the question of the day.

Ever since the Union the Catholic question had been a subject of trouble to Administrations. The Act of Union had, undoubtedly, been made acceptable to many Catholics of rank and influence by the promise that it should be but a first step to Catholic Emancipation. Pitt did, in fact, bring in a Bill for the relief of the Catholics in 1801, but the King would not hear of it. Pitt and his friends resigned office. Many people were strongly of opinion then, and since, that Pitt had determined to go out of office for a while on whatever pretext. The English public were beginning to be sick of the long war against the French, which was costing so much money and so much blood, and in which many English taxpayers, oppressed by burdens of taxation, were beginning to find that they had very little interest.

Pitt, it was said, foresaw clearly enough that a peace of some sort would undoubtedly be patched up, and saw, too, that such a peace would not last. On both grounds, therefore—because he did not approve of a peace just then, and because he was convinced that a peace made then would not last—he was determined to have nothing to do with the transaction. He looked about—this is the contention—for some plausible excuse to resign office, knowing he could return to it whenever he pleased. He remembered his pledges to the Irish Catholics, and, knowing perfectly well that the King would never consent to Catholic Emancipation, he went through the form of attempting to fulfil his promises. The King was obstinate, and Pitt resigned. The Treaty of Amiens was made, and proved a hopeless failure. The voice of the country summoned Pitt back to power. He came back, and promised the King never to disturb the royal conscience or the royal temper again by any allusion to the claims of the Roman Catholics.

Whether this explanation of Pitt's conduct be true or not, it is certain that he returned to office under a pledge not to distress the King any more about Catholic Emancipation. In that condition the whole subject of controversy remained down to the time when Robert Peel went over to Dublin Castle. The understanding was that nothing was to be done or attempted in the direction of Catholic Emancipation. This principle suited Peel in every way. He was at that time, and had always been, a sincere and uncompromising opponent of the admission of the Catholics to political equality. That feeling had with him all the depth and strength of a religious principle. There was something almost Puritanical in the sternness of his devotion to what he believed to be one of the cardinal principles of Protestantism. The fact cannot be too strongly affirmed, because we shall never appreciate all that was most magnanimous and statesmanlike in Peel's character if we allow ourselves to fall into the belief of nearly all his enemies, and some of his friends, that he took up lightly certain principles merely because he was, if we may so describe it, born into them, and that, with the growth of time and thought and experience, he naturally grew out of them—they fell from him, and he was free. To appreciate the sacrifice that Peel made to his convictions of the present, we must appreciate the strength and fervour of his convictions of the past.

Peel opposed Grattan's measure of Catholic relief in 1810—Grattan had come back to public life to be the champion of the Roman Catholics, staunch Protestant though he was—and Sir Henry Parnell's motion on the same subject, two years after. Not merely did he oppose these measures, but he made by far the ablest of the speeches delivered against them. The extreme Tories all over the country were positively delighted with him, and hailed him as the rising star of the Church party in Parliament. Canning had already declared himself openly in favour of the Catholic claims, and had even made a motion for an inquiry into the nature of the laws affecting them. It was beginning to be found impossible to get together any strong Administration without admitting to it some men who, like Canning, were openly in favour of Catholic Emancipation. Therefore, in the Government of Lord Liverpool it was understood that the question was to be left open. The Ministry would take no step in favour of Catholic relief; but it was not to be a reason for excluding a man from the Cabinet that he was personally in favour of Emancipation. This fact, too, made Peel's star shine all the brighter in the eyes of the uncompromising Tories. He was looked upon as the head of the party who would, sooner or later, have to do battle against Canning.

But, of course, these facts, well known in Ireland, were not likely to secure for Peel a favourable reception there. He was instantly nicknamed 'Orange Peel' by the followers of O'Connell. Nor did he receive very much more favour from the extreme opponents of O'Connell. Notwithstanding the nickname of Orange Peel, the new Chief Secretary was not in any sense an Orangeman. The Orangemen were, for their numbers, nearly as great a trouble to each succeeding Government as the Catholics. The Irish Orangemen—or, perhaps, it would be better to say the Orangemen in Ireland—out-Eldoned Eldon himself in the bitterness of their hatred to everything Catholic and everything progressive. To give satisfaction to some of these men, Peel should have done nothing short of dispersing the Catholic meeting by some prompt whiffs of grape-shot, and ordering the immediate execution of O'Connell. Peel saw his way clearly. He would not depart from that way to win the cheers of the Orangemen, any more than he would to win the cheers of the Catholics. His desire and his determination were to hold a perfectly impartial course; to touch nothing which had to do with Catholic relief or which could give the least hope of any measure in that direction, but in all other ways to promote administrative reform and the development of education. He re-organised, or, rather, indeed, created the Irish police force. He made earnest efforts for the increase of public schools. He worked hard, and did so in many directions. His Lancashire bringing-up, and his business habits, stood him in good stead. His colleagues and subordinates in Dublin Castle were amazed, amused; some, even, were not a little scandalised at the manner in which the new Secretary toiled away through hours and hours. It was not in keeping with the traditions—of the office, some men thought,—to give up all that time to dull, dry duty. What about the lounges into the club, the gallops in the Phoenix Park, the long rides by the side of some open carriage with a coronet on its panel, and a pretty woman on its cushions? What about the games of whist, and all the other amusements which brighten and shorten the day of the oppressed official? Peel was setting a bad example, Dublin Castle thought.

Peel worked away after his own fashion, and did not take the slightest notice of ordinary gossip about him; perhaps never heard of it. What happened to him in Dublin was what happened to him in London, and wherever he went. Those who knew him well, were charmed with him; those who did not know him well, misunderstood him, and therefore were disposed to dislike him. He was, indeed, a man who must be known intimately, or cannot be known at all.

Peel and O'Connell came to an open quarrel. Hard words had been interchanged, and a challenge was sent and accepted. But there was some delay in settling the conditions of the meeting, and the authorities got wind of the affair, and intervened; and, in the expressive words of Mr Foker's groom, in *Pendennis*, 'Fight didn't come off.' In those days still lingered the tradition that it was the business and the duty of a public man to sustain his words with his pistol. It is a somewhat curious fact that the last serious talk of a duel between two members of Parliament, the last project of a duel with which the House of Commons interfered, was one between another Sir Robert Peel, son of the subject of this memoir, and a then popular Irish politician, The O'Donoghue. But that which was a mere absurdity or scandal in the days of the present Sir Robert Peel, was the right sort of thing in the early days of his father. We have seen that just before this Canning went out with Lord Castlereagh. Long after this Disraeli challenged O'Connell.

III

'The Chain of the Catholic'

Peel resigns office and becomes known as a great financier—Supports Lord Liverpool's repressive policy—Death of George III—Succession of George IV— The Reform movement—The proceedings against Queen Caroline

PEEL HELD ON TO HIS uncongenial duties for about six years. They must have been to him thoroughly irksome, except, of course, those by which he was enabled to re-organise defective systems of administration. In 1818 he resigned the office of Chief Secretary to the Lord Lieutenant. In the meantime many things had happened. The long war with France was over and done. Napoleon had gone down, never to rise again. The Congress of Vienna, and the 'crowned conspirators of Verona,' had settled the map of Europe to their satisfaction for a time. The eyes of the English public were withdrawn from the battle-fields of armies on the Continent to the battle-fields of parties and of factions here at home. The defects and errors of the Liverpool and Castlereagh Administration were becoming more and more evident. Perhaps already, during his experience of Ireland, Peel had begun to have a glimmering consciousness that peace and order are not to be secured by mere measures of repression. At least, we can see that some such assumption is warranted by Peel's subsequent course of action with regard to the Roman Catholic claims. So far as English policy was concerned, he remained the same inflexible Tory that he had been before. But he was, for some reason, anxious to get free of the Liverpool Administration just then. He resigned his Irish office, and did not accept any other. So entirely was he regarded still as the leader of the Tory party in the House of Commons that, when the retirement of Mr Abbott from the Speaker's chair, and his elevation to the peerage, left a vacancy in the representation of the University of Oxford, Peel was invited to stand as a candidate. It is certain that Canning himself had a strong ambition to represent the University but the whole influence of Lord Eldon was given to Peel, and Peel was elected. Canning took the preference given to his friend and rival with dignity and sweetness, and congratulated Peel on his election. In 1816 he had consented to accept the office of President of the Board of Control.

A stormy time was now coming on for the Government. There was widespread distress. There were riots in the counties of England arising out of the distress. There were riots in various parts of London. Secret Committees were appointed by both Houses of the Legislature to inquire into the alleged disaffection of part of the people. The Habeas Corpus Act was suspended. The march of the Blanketeers from Manchester caused panic and consternation through various circles in London. The march of the Blanketeers was a very simple and harmless project. A large number of the working-men in Manchester conceived the idea of walking to London to lay an account of their distress before the heads of the Government, and to ask that some remedy might be found, and also to appeal for the granting of Parliamentary reform. It was part of their arrangement that each man should carry a blanket with him, as they would, necessarily, have to sleep at many places along the way, and they were not exactly in funds to pay for first-class hotel accommodation. The nickname of Blanketeers was given to them because of their portable sleeping arrangements. The whole project was simple, was touching in its simplicity. Even at this distance of time one cannot read about it without being moved by its pathetic childishness. These poor men thought they had nothing to do but to walk to London, and get to speech of Lord Liverpool, and justice would be done to them and their claims. The Government of Lord Liverpool dealt very roundly, and in a very different way, with the Blanketeers. If the poor men had been marching on London with pikes, muskets, and swords, they could not have created a greater fury of panic and of passion in official circles. The Government, availing itself of the suspension of the Habeas Corpus Act, had the leaders of the movement captured and sent to prison, stopped the march by military force, and dispersed those who were taking part in it. The poor Blanketeers were more lucky, however, than the men who went to Versailles to represent their poverty and their claims to the King, and whose leaders were promptly taken and hanged for their impertinence. The 'Massacre of Peterloo,' as it is not inappropriately called, took place not long after. A great public meeting was held at St Peter's Field, then on the outskirts of Manchester, now the site of the Free Trade Hall, which many years later rang so often to the thrilling tones of John Bright. The meeting was called to petition for Parliamentary reform. It should be remembered that in those days Manchester, Birmingham, and other great cities were without any manner of representation in Parliament. It was a vast meeting—some eighty thousand men and women are stated to have been present. The yeomanry, for some reason impossible to understand, endeavoured to disperse the meeting, and actually dashed in upon the crowd, spurring their horses and flourishing their sabres. Eleven persons were killed, and several hundreds were wounded. The Government brought in, as their panacea for popular trouble and discontent, the famous Six Acts. These Acts were simply measures to render it more easy for the authorities to put down or disperse meetings which they considered objectionable, and to suppress any manner of publication which they chose to call seditious. But among them were some Bills to prevent training and drilling, and the collection and use of arms. These measures show what the panic of the Government was. It was the conviction of the ruling classes that the poor and the working-classes of England were preparing a revolution. Some inner promptings of conscience may have suggested this fear. Men in authority may have observed that in other countries revolution had been attempted with no greater provocation to stimulate it. Indeed, it now appears all but certain that a long-protracted administration of the policy of Liverpool and Castlereagh, and a denial of the claim to Parliamentary reform, must have plunged England into the throes of a revolution. During all this time, the few genuine Radicals in the House of Commons were bringing on motion after motion for Parliamentary reform, just as Grattan and his friends were bringing forward motion after motion for Catholic Emancipation. In 1818, a motion by Sir Francis Burdett for annual Parliaments and universal suffrage was lost by a majority of 106 to nobody. How, it may be asked, could this possibly come about? Why did not even the member who brought forward the motion condescend to vote for it, or, if he did not mean to vote for it, why did he challenge a division? It happened in this way, as persons familiar with the usages of the House of Commons will guess. The motion had only two supporters—Burdett himself, and his colleague, Lord Cochrane, who, after an unjust imprisonment and an unmerited degradation, had come back to the House of Commons. The forms of the House require two tellers on either side, and a compliance with this inevitable rule took up the whole strength of Burdett's party. In such a case now we should say that into the 'Aye' lobby— that in favour of Burdett's motion—nobody walked; for the very good reason that there was nobody to walk.

Peel was out of office all this time. But he gave a strong support to the measures of the Government. He supported the Six Acts, and he approved of the conduct of Ministers with regard to the events of Peterloo. So far his antique Toryism had moulted no feather. He did not, however, give up the best of his abilities to the support of measures like the Six Acts. He began to be known as a great authority on finance and a far-seeing financial reformer. He delivered about this time some of the most impressive and some of the most important speeches of his public career. He was in strong sympathy with the views of the economical party, whose opinions were treated with a lofty scorn by most of the official statesmen of the day. Francis Homer had been at the head of the Economist party until his premature death, and Peel cordially recognised his talents and admired his principles. The entrance of David Ricardo into the House of Commons gave further strength to the Economists. A signal tribute to the financial capacity of Robert Peel was given in 1819.   A Committee of the House was appointed to consider the question of a resumption of cash payments, and some kindred questions arising out of the financial and commercial troubles and convulsions which attend on the passing from a state of war into a state of peace, the fictitious and unnatural semblance of prosperous trade which the state of war brings up, collapsing the moment it comes in contrast with the cold, clear dawn of peace. The exhila-ration of the night of revel is succeeded by the chill morning, and the painful necessity of encountering the prosaic, inevitable details of the day's duty. Peel was appointed chairman of this Committee—and what a Committee it was. It almost takes one's breath away to read that list of names: Canning, Castlereagh, Sir James Mackintosh, Huskisson, Vansittart, Tierney; and over these Robert Peel, then only thirty-one years of age, took the presiding place. It fell to his duty in May, 1819, to move resolutions recommending a return to cash payments. He declared himself the advocate and the champion of 'the old, the vulgar doctrine, as some people have called it, that the true standard of value consisted in a definite quantity of gold bullion.' He insisted on it that 'a certain weight of gold bullion with an impression on it denoting it to be of that certain weight, and of a certain fineness, constituted the only true, intelligible, and adequate standard of value.' The House of Commons acted on Peel's recommendations; but it is curious to note that Sir Robert Peel, the father and political tutor of the great rising statesman, took a different view. Peel's proposals were embodied in an Act of Parliament.

On January 29, 1820, the long reign of George III came to an end. The life of the King closed in darkness of eyes and mind. Stone-blind, stone-deaf, and, except for rare lucid intervals, wholly out of his senses, the poor old King wandered from room to room of his palace, a touching picture, with his long, white, flowing beard, now repeating to himself the awful words of Milton— the 'dark, dark, dark, amid the blaze of noon—irrecoverably dark'—now, in a happier mood, announcing himself to be in the companionship of angels.

George, the Prince Regent, succeeded, of course, to the throne; and George IV at once announced his willingness to retain the services of the Ministry of Lord Liverpool. The Whigs had at one time expected much from the coming of George IV to the throne, but their hopes had begun to be chilled of late. The Irish Catholics still, and for yet a little time longer, looked to him with confidence for a redress of their great grievance. George IV paid a visit to Ireland shortly after his accession to the throne, and was received with almost frantic delight by O'Connell and other leaders of the Irish Catholics, and, indeed, by the population generally. There was a wild hope that George was returning to his long-forsaken Liberal principles, and that he would favour the scheme of Catholic Emancipation. George himself indirectly and tacitly encouraged the idea, although by a sort of common understanding no allusion whatever was made to the subject. The King returned to London very soon, and it was discovered before long that nothing was to come of his Irish visit, except the erection of a singularly ugly obelisk, and the changing of the name of Dunleary to that of Kingstown.

Peel took little part in the debates concerning the Bill of pains and penalties against the unfortunate Queen Caroline which was brought in by the Government of Lord Liverpool. We need not go into the long story of the charges made against the wife of George IV, the proceedings that were taken in consequence, and the wild agitation which was aroused all over the country. Canning advised and defended the Queen; Brougham threw his whole soul and his whole passion into her cause. The feeling against the Bill ran so high that it had to be dropped, and the public rejoicings over its abandonment amounted to actual exultation. Peel opposed a vote of censure on the Ministry for their action with regard to the Queen, although he carefully guarded himself against expressing approval of everything they had done. It was a troublous time. The King was very unpopular. He was shot at one night when driving to one of the theatres; two bullets broke the glass in the carriage windows. The famous Cato Street Conspiracy to assassinate the leading members of the Government was discovered, and the chiefs of the conspiracy were tried, convicted, and promptly hanged. In the meantime, the efforts of the few reformers in Parliament were as zealous and resolute as if these men were incapable of being made to believe that their cause was hopeless. Everybody in society everywhere said that their agitation was mere midsummer madness; but they held on in the confidence of the justness of their cause. Plunket, an Irishman almost as eloquent as Grattan himself, had succeeded, on Grattan's death in 1820, to his place as Parliamentary leader of the advocates of Catholic Emancipation. To that cause Canning had in the House of Commons given his open adhesion. Sir James Mackintosh was fighting hard to obtain some mitigation of the terrible penal code which made almost every offence punishable by death. The Catholic cause was distinctly advancing; it was gradually winning over the House of Commons, although even still Robert Peel declared himself against its principle just as strongly as ever. But the cause of Parliamentary reform seemed to make no advance. It had now, however, a new and zealous champion, in the person of Lord John Russell. Lord John Russell came quietly into the movement. He was destined to be of infinitely greater service to it than Burdett or Cochrane or even than Brougham himself.

Peel—Russell—Canning

Lord John Russell and Robert Peel were to be rivals and antagonists during a long series of years. In character, in conditions of life, as well as in
political views, they were curiously contrasted. Russell was the scion of one
of the greatest families in England; great in its far-reaching pedigree, and
greater still in the illustrious character of many of its members. Russell had
had but an imperfect education, in the scholastic or schoolmaster's sense of
the word. In classic attainments, and, indeed, in general literary culture, he
could not be compared for a moment with Peel. But he had a much more
extensive knowledge of the world and of continental politics than had fallen
to the lot of Peel. He had begun travelling very young, and had been led
into scenes memorable for ever in the history of England. He had again and
again visited the English camping-grounds during the great Peninsular War.
He had hung on the rough edge of battle. He had ridden along the British
lines with Sir Arthur Wellesley, afterwards to be the Duke of Wellington.
He had visited Napoleon in Elba, and had heard Napoleon declare, with a
sigh, that war was a splendid game; and he had tried to explain to the fallen
Emperor that there was not the slightest likelihood of Wellington trying to
seize the English Crown. He had known Metternich and Talleyrand, and,
indeed, must have known, even in his earlier days, almost everyone worth
knowing in Europe. He had been brought up among statesmen, and great
nobles, and philosophers, and poets. He had large and liberal tastes, and
he loved to hear the talk of gifted and famous men and women. He had sat

as a child at the feet of Fox, and had talked at Florence with the widow of Charles Edward, 'the Young Chevalier.' He was eclectic in his literary and artistic tastes, and he tried verse-writing, novel-writing, play-writing, and showed some aptitude in each branch of literature. Some of his smaller and lighter poems are bright and pretty,—and far above the level of the ordinary old-fashioned 'Verses by A Person of Quality.' But his chief passion was for politics; the House of Commons was his natural arena. He was sent into the House, by the influence of his family, before he had quite come of age. The same thing had happened to Fox. Nobody troubled to call attention to the fact, and it passed over without any intervention of Parliamentary laws. Russell was, in fact, abroad when his election to Parliament took place. He had early shown himself a true descendant of his great Whig family. If Peel was born a Tory, Russell was surely born a Whig. He did not at first very much like the House of Commons. Its Toryism made him despondent, and he at one time talked of giving up political life altogether. He was dissuaded, however, by his friends, Thomas Moore, the Irish poet, being one of the most energetic in his remonstrances, both in poetry and in prose. Russell made up his mind to remain in Parliament. He could not have left it, although he seems to have been perfectly sincere at the time in his desire to do so. It was his appointed ground, and he had to stay there and fight his long course. He and Peel, unlike in so many other ways, had two points of resemblance. Each was so shy as to seem cold, reserved, and proud to outsiders; and each had an exalted sense of duty, and a lofty, disinterested, and unselfish spirit.

Russell soon came to be regarded in Parliament as the hope of the Whigs, as Peel was the hope of the Tories. He devoted himself from the outset to the cause of Religious Liberty and Parliamentary Reform. Of course, he kept clear of the more extreme and wilder schemes of the few Radicals who were then in the House of Commons, and whose wildest and most extreme schemes have nearly all, it may be said, been the law of the land these years and years back. But at that time, and to men brought up as Russell had been brought up, they seemed crude, far-off, and impracticable, and he could not give them much countenance. His style of speaking was usually somewhat cold and monotonous at first, but as he went on he showed that he had genuine debating power of a very high order, and as much eloquence as could be given by admirably pointed argument and remarkably felicitous expression. He wanted the fire which, whether subdued or allowed to flame, is essential to the genius of the real orator. But if he was not a born orator, he was a born debater. He was very quick at repartee, and clever in sarcastic phraseology. In short, he was a man to be contrasted with Peel, and compared with Peel. One surpassed in this quality, and the other in that; but they stood on much the same level, and were fitting and worthy antagonists.

As early as 1819 Russell had brought forward resolutions in the House of Commons in favour of Parliamentary Reform, which were, of course, defeated. These resolutions were very moderate; they merely called upon the House to affirm that all boroughs found guilty of gross and notorious bribery and corruption should be disfranchised, and that the representation should be transferred to some large boroughs or great counties; that steps should be taken to inquire into the extent of bribery and corruption; and that the borough of Grampound, just convicted of gross and notorious bribery and corruption, and whose representative had been fined and sent to prison, should be disfranchised. Lord Castlereagh got up at once and offered a sort of compromise. He said that if Lord John Russell would withdraw his resolutions, and bring in a Bill to disfranchise the borough of Grampound, the Government would put no difficulty in his way. Russell accepted the offer, and withdrew his resolutions. The incident is well worth mentioning, as the first movement made towards electoral and Parliamentary reform by Lord John Russell.

In January, 1822, Lord Sidmouth retired from office, and Peel succeeded him as Home Secretary. The recent course of events had seemed on the whole to be favourable to the Tories. The Cato Street Conspiracy had horrified the public mind, and had turned many people of not irrational mood against any popular movement. It was absurd, of course, to discover any relationship between legitimate constitutional movement for reform and the wild schemes of assassins; but with the nation the first effect of political crime is always to discourage and discredit popular movement. That is the first effect; after a while cool reflection again asserts its sway, and people who are capable of thinking at all begin to ask themselves whether the crime itself was not but a symptom of a condition of things in the political framework of society which called for remedy rather than repression.

For the moment, however, the position seemed decidedly in favour of the Tories, so far as any reform movement was concerned. In the session of 1822 Lord John Russell brought forward a very moderate resolution, declaring that 'the present state of representation requires serious consideration.' The resolution was rejected by a majority of 105 votes. Later in the session Brougham brought forward a motion declaring that 'the influence of the Crown is destructive of the independence of Parliament,' and that that influence 'has largely increased since Dunning's resolution in 1780.' The resolution referred to was the famous motion, carried in 17890 by Mr Dunning, the great advocate, afterwards Lord Ashburton, which declared that 'the power of the

Crown has increased, is increasing, and ought to be diminished.' That resolution was carried by a majority of 18. Brougham's was rejected by a majority of 115. But the Catholic question was distinctly advancing. In the same session (1822) Canning brought in a Bill to admit Catholic peers to sit in the House of Lords. The Bill passed through the Commons, and was only rejected in the House of Lords by a majority of 42.

On the 12th of August, 1822, the world was horrified by the news that Lord Castlereagh had committed suicide. Canning had already received the appointment of Governor-General of India, and was actually about to start for Calcutta. It was thought necessary, however, that he should be invited to take the office of Foreign Secretary, which the death of Castlereagh had left vacant, and he accepted the invitation, and renounced the more splendid and lucrative position which had been given to him. The Government was thereupon divided into what might properly be called two sections or parties—one under Canning, and the other under Peel. Peel led those who still accepted the wisdom of Lord Eldon—'the unbending Tories,' as Macaulay called them at a later date. Canning was the leader of those who advocated Catholic Emancipation. As regards other questions, there was little and lessening difference of opinion between Peel and Canning. Peel was well disposed to accept the bold and liberal foreign policy of his colleague; Canning was quite advanced enough as an economist to follow the widening financial views of Peel. Peel was much occupied just then with the measures of financial reform which were caused by the disturbed and distressed condition of the country. Peel passed his Currency Bill. Huskisson, who had become President of the Board of Trade, carried his Reciprocity Duties Bill, which much mitigated the effect of the Navigation Laws. It is not true that there was anything unsatisfactory in the relations between Peel and Canning. Peel had the most generous admiration for the genius and the character of Canning. A little later on Peel told one of his relatives that, when he went down to a Cabinet Council with some matter of great importance in his mind, and his own ideas made up as to what ought to be done concerning it, he generally found himself anticipated by Canning in the very view of the subject which he himself had taken—found Canning advancing the very reasons on which he had himself proceeded, 'clothed,' Peel added, 'in better language than any into which I could have put them.' It would, indeed, be impossible that these two men should not have come to appreciate each other thoroughly if time had been spared to both of them. Time was not spared to Canning.

In 1827 Lord Liverpool became seriously ill, and felt that he could not continue in office. The question then arose, What was to be done? Could the Government be carried on under the leadership of a man of such commanding influence as the Duke of Wellington—a Government on the old, unbending Tory principles, pledged more or less to resist every reform? No, there did not seem much chance for such an Administration. The great difficulty was the Catholic question, and the majority of the House of Commons had by this time become educated on the Catholic question. Only the King and the House of Lords really stood out on the old lines of unqualified resistance. It seemed, then, almost out of the question to think of setting up such a Ministry, with any hope of its keeping up when it had been set up; and there did not seem much to be gained by setting up a Ministry that must incontinently tumble down again. Under such conditions, every eye was naturally turned on Canning. The King did not like the idea of accepting Canning as his Prime Minister. He chafed at it a good deal; but it had to be done. The King sent for Canning, and invited him to form an Administration in which Catholic Emancipation was to be an open question, but which was to be pledged to oppose any movement for Parliamentary reform. Canning consented, and was quite consistent in doing so. He considered that a great step had been gained when the King went so far as to allow Catholic Emancipation to be an open question, and he was in agreement with Wellington and Peel on the subject of Parliamentary reform. But his difficulties were only beginning. The Duke of Wellington and Lord Eldon determined to have nothing to do with the new Administration, and Robert Peel went with them. It is not likely that Peel would have taken such a step if left to himself. His differences of opinion with Canning were not nearly so great as they had been. He no longer acknowledged himself to be an inveterate Tory, set against all progressive movements, and opposed in principle to all reform. Again and again, in his speeches in the House of Commons, he had given it to be understood that he was prepared to consider measures on their own merits, and not according to some *a priori* principle of judgment. He was opposed to the kind of Parliamentary reform which Russell and Lambton, the celebrated Lord Durham of a later day, and Brougham and Burdett, were continually bringing forward. But he had passed away altogether from the stone-hatchet period of political life. As regards the Catholic question, he must already have begun to see clearly enough that things could not long remain in their existing condition. There would not seem to have been any strong reason, therefore, why he should not accept office with Canning. But the whole question was settled for him when Wellington and Eldon refused to form part of the new Cabinet. It was merely a choice between two courses; to go with Wellington, or to go with Canning. Every sentiment of loyalty impelled Peel the one way. Had he broken away from Wellington, he would have seemed to be breaking away from his party; and he had no intention of breaking away from his party. He was a devoted friend to the Duke of Wellington, and had a great personal regard for Lord Eldon. He made up his mind quickly, and refused to cooperate with Canning. There was nothing then left for Canning to do but to court the assistance of the Whigs. But the Whigs were divided among themselves. Some of them would have nothing to do with the Canning Administration. Lord Grey, Lord Althorp, and others, were of this mind; while Lord John Russell, on the other hand, was so pleased to see Canning at the head of the Government that he declared himself not unwilling for the moment to refrain from pressing forward the question of Parliamentary reform. Some of the Whigs consented to join Canning. Lord Eldon was succeeded in the office of Lord Chancellor by Lord Lyndhurst, and Peel became the recognised leader of the Opposition in the House of Commons.

The Canning Administration lasted but a very short time. It was broken up by the death of Canning himself; on August 8, 1827, almost immediately after his accession to the position of Prime Minister. Canning's health had long been giving way, and the strain and stress of the life of office and the House of Commons were too much for him. He never had any great physical or constitutional strength, and his was an eager and a sensitive spirit, not over well-suited at the best for the wear and tear, the fierce faction fights, of English public life. He was unsparing of himself in debate, as, indeed, it must be owned that he was unsparing of others as well. He was as strenuous a combatant as Disraeli in later times, and he had little of that robust endurance, that proud patience which distinguished Disraeli. After the death of Canning an attempt was made to carry on his principle of administration by Lord Goderich, but the attempt was not a success. The equipoise was too delicate and too difficult to be long maintained; certainly too difficult to be long maintained by a Minister of the moderate capacity and influence of Lord Goderich.

The place had not yet been found for a really Liberal Administration; and there was no way open for anything effective in the way of compromise, Lord Goderich soon threw up the task, and there was nothing for it but to fall back upon the Duke of Wellington and an avowed Tory Administration. The task to be solved was how to govern England without any regard to the voice of the English people.

The Duke of Wellington had far too much good sense to be very confident in his capacity to accomplish such a feat; but when his master sent for him, and asked him to undertake the work, he could only answer with the simple American soldier described by Nathaniel Hawthorne, 'Sir, I will try.' Then, and at all other times, the Duke of Wellington regarded himself merely as a soldier of the Crown, and his one great object was to see that the Government of the King was carried on. He accepted office, therefore, in the face of the great rising trouble about Reform and the already active trouble about Catholic Emancipation. One little sign of a recognition of coming change was given in the fact that Lord Lyndhurst, who had been Lord Chancellor under Mr Canning and Lord Goderich, was continued in his office, and that Lord Eldon, whose views admitted of no compromise, was not invited to return to the woolsack.

Peel became Home Secretary once again. Huskisson was Secretary for War and the Colonies. Lord Palmerston was Secretary at War. Lord John Russell brought forward his motion for a repeal of the Test and Corporation Acts. The Test and Corporation Acts directed all officers, civil and military, under Government, to receive the sacrament according to the forms of the Church of England, and made similar provision for corporate officials. The first Act was passed in 1673, but its rigours were mitigated in 1727 by a yearly Act of Indemnity for all Dissenters who might have held office contrary to its provisions. One of the great arguments of those who sustained the disqualifying Acts was that these measures did no real harm to anybody after the passing of the Bill of Annual Indemnity. A Dissenter, it was urged, might hold an office to which he had been elected, and was only put to the nominal trouble of availing himself of the provisions of the Bill of Indemnity. On the other hand, it was reasonably contended that the passing of the Indemnity Act rendered the Test Act absolutely useless for the purposes which those who passed it had in view. It could no longer shut out Dissenters; it could only impose on them an offensive and a futile badge of religious inferiority. They had to ask the forgiveness of Parliament for their impertinence in accepting offices which a member of the State Church was free to accept without the permission of anybody but those who elected him. It was an insult to Dissent, and it was no protection to the Church, even if it were supposed that the Church needed any such protection, or could be protected in such a way. Lord John Russell carried his motion in the House of Commons by a majority of 237 to 193, and a measure founded on his motion was passed by both Houses and became law on May 9, 1828. The old order was changing, giving place to new.

The great battle about religious disqualification had yet to be fought. The agitation for Catholic Emancipation began to swell to portentous proportions in Ireland. O'Connell, Sheil, and other prominent men in Irish politics were at the head of the movement. The Catholic Association had been formed in Ireland to carry on the agitation. An Act was passed in 1825 ordaining its suppression for three years. The Association, however, could not really be suppressed. At least, if it disappeared under one name, it instantly rose to the surface under another. Nothing was more easy than to start a fresh association with a new title; or, rather, indeed, to carry on the old Association under a new title. If the new name were objectionable, nothing was more easy than to hold a series of public meetings not bearing the name of any association. O'Connell was a master of every art, and craft, and stratagem by which to defeat the absurd and hopeless policy of the Administration. The agitation spread like wildfire; all the King's horses and all the King's men could not prevent the conflagration from extending over the country. In truth, the policy of Catholic disqualification had come to be an anomaly and an anachronism.

Peel had to consider how the new conditions were to be met. No part of his public conduct, except, perhaps, his action later with regard to Free Trade, was more sharply criticised by some of his former friends and colleagues than the resolution to which he finally came on the subject of Catholic Emancipation. He found on coming into office that the Catholic Association, under one name or other, in one form or other, had taken fast hold of the whole Catholic population of Ireland. He found also, that it had the sympathy of all the Liberals of England. The Act for the suppression of the Catholic Association was just about to expire, its time having run out. What was the proper course to be pursued? Peel, as Home Secretary, was responsible for the government of Ireland. On him lay, or would lie, the final reproach if things were to go wrong in Ireland. He had taken office at the express request of the Duke of Wellington. The moment the Duke received a summons to attend the King, and had from the King's own mouth an invitation to form a Government, he sent to Peel, and told George IV that he relied on Peel's co-operation, and that he would see no one and consult with no one on the subject until he had talked with Peel. It may be mentioned that the King told Wellington that the new Administration ought to be composed of persons of both opinions with regard to the Catholic question, and that he had no objection to anybody except Lord Grey. There was *carte blanche* for the Duke, as the Duke himself expressed it to Peel, with the exception of one man. That one man was a statesman and a patriot of the purest character and the highest political purpose. The King would have anybody except Lord Grey.

It will be seen that the statesmen of that day had to struggle with a sort of difficulty against which it is understood that the more fortunate statesmen of our time have not to contend. The personal likings and dislikings of the sovereign had to be considered first of all. For a long term of years in the time of

George III and George IV, the burning question of Catholic Emancipation had to be kept out of sight because these sovereigns had an objection to hearing it talked about. The whims of the King had to be consulted and allowed for as if they were the whims of some spoilt *prima donna* whose manager has to humour her at any cost. The King will not hear of this measure—the King will not hear of that measure—the King will not have this man—the King will not part with that man; such were the difficulties with which the statesmen of those days had to put up. Nor had they merely to put up with them they had to make them a part of all their political plans and calculations. A great Minister might see his way clear and bright before him to the accomplishment of some momentous reform; he might have convinced himself thoroughly that the reform was needed for the peace and the prosperity of the country; he might have had the most conclusive evidence that the vast majority of the people would welcome it with rapture—but then, what of all this? The King did not like it—the King would not listen to any talk about it—it would be useless to propose it now—we must only wait—we must only wait. No doubt, in the end the King gave way. In most cases, at least, he gave way in sulky, sullen anger, after almost hysterical outbursts of passion. He had to be coerced into giving way, as a stubborn child has to be coerced into taking the medicine that is good for him. Anything more unkingly than the scenes between the Kings and the Ministers at this period of our history it is hardly possible to conceive.

The King, then, would not have Lord Grey on any terms; and he would not have Catholic Emancipation made a Cabinet question. It was to remain open; perhaps it would vanish, or be swallowed up by the earth, if only it were left alone for a while. In any case, happen what would, the King insisted that there must be a Protestant Lord Chancellor, a Protestant Lord Lieutenant, and a Protestant Lord Chancellor of Ireland. On these conditions the Duke of Wellington was free to do the best he could.

Peel was by no means anxious to come back to office; at all events, he was unwilling to come back to office at that time. This was not because he shrank in the least from the responsibility of any position in which he could act on the best inspiration of his own judgment. He was not a man to hold back because of any feeling of that kind. But he had grave doubts as to whether, under all the peculiar conditions of the times—and the will of the Sovereign among the rest of them—he could really do any good. We have the fullest and most candid accounts of all his opinions and feelings at three great stages of his public career in the Memoirs which he left behind him, and which were published after his death by his trustees, the late Lord

Stanhope and the late Lord Cardwell. If ever a statesman did his best to put posterity in a condition to judge of him and his motives at each crisis in his public life, Peel certainly is entitled to that praise. For those who take any real interest in politics and the growth of political ideas, there is hardly any reading more fascinating than these letters and memoranda, which lay bare to us the whole working of Peel's intellect and conscience, and show us how ideas germinated in his mind, and at last grew up into blossom and fruit.

V

The Clare Election

The Catholic question burning—Peel studies the question, and recognises facts—The Clare election, its meaning and its consequences—Lord Anglesey's views—Peel begins to see his way

PEEL TELLS US HOW, ON the one hand, it appeared to him that the attempt to form a united Government on the principle of resistance to the claims of the Roman Catholics was perfectly hopeless. 'In the preceding year the measure of concession had been negatived in the House of Commons, by a majority of four votes only, by a very full House.' Peel, it will be observed, through all his career kept taking account of the votes of the House of Commons, as the pilot takes his soundings. He knew perfectly well that, however the House of Lords or the Sovereign might resist for a time, the decision of the House of Commons must prevail in the end. That House was, indeed, very imperfect as a representative institution at the time; but still, it was a representative institution of some sort, and the House of Lords was not, and the Sovereign was not. Peel was a man of the highest principles; but he was not, and never could be, a political fanatic. He never could make a fetish of some partisan article of faith. He never believed himself to have started into political life with all the full outfit of idea and information which he was ever to need or to obtain. He did not suppose that he had set out on his new career with a store, like the bridal *trousseau* of a Swiss girl, which was to last a whole lifetime. He did not, it must be owned, look far ahead. He had not time for scanning the political horizon with a field-glass. He was no star-gazer. He was content to wait until a political question came up, and justified its title to consideration. But when a political question did thus come up, he was utterly in capable of the weakness that would close its eyes to realities, and go on as if nothing had happened. No new fact could come up so serious, so formidable, or so portentous, that Peel would not find himself able to confront it and put it to question.

He found, then, that a Government could no longer be held together on the principle of resistance to the claims of the Catholics. This was not a welcome fact to Peel, who still retained his old objections to Catholic Emancipation; but there was the fact, and he accepted it. He was anxious, therefore, that a chance should be given to some of Canning's friends who had left Lord Liverpool's Administration, and that they should be invited to take office under the Duke of Wellington. He was not, in his heart, very sanguine of any great good to come even from that; but he felt sure that the effort ought to be made—that the experiment ought to be tried. In accordance with his suggestion, therefore, Lord Palmerston, Huskisson, and one or two other Canningites, became members of the Duke of Wellington's Cabinet. William Lamb, afterwards Lord Melbourne, a friend of Canning's, who had not been in Lord Liverpool's Administration, promised to lend his assistance to the new Government. But Peel was not hopeful. He did not yet see his way to the granting of Catholic Emancipation; but he saw more and more clearly, day by day, the tremendous difficulty of resisting the demand. The moment the Ministry was formed—the moment, indeed, that he saw it in a fair way to formation—he set himself down to the task of examining keenly and critically into the whole condition of Ireland.

The Marquis of Wellesley, elder brother of the Duke or Wellington,—who would have been historically famous if his renown had not been overshadowed by that of his brother,—had been for seven years Lord Lieutenant of Ireland. He was in favour of Catholic Emancipation, and had brought forward a motion in its support in the House of Lords. He had remained in office during the Administration of Canning and that of Lord Goderich. But when the Duke of Wellington entered on his task of government with the announcement that Catholic Emancipation was not to be a Cabinet measure, Lord Wellesley felt that he could no longer continue to hold his place in Dublin Castle. He resigned his office, and was succeeded by Lord Anglesey. Lord Anglesey had been a brilliant cavalry officer in the wars against Napoleon, had been commander of the English cavalry in Flanders, and had done splendid service at Waterloo. While he was in Parliament he had talked violently and wildly about Irish agitation, and the feasibility of putting it down by a few indiscriminate charges of cavalry. It was believed then by many, that when Lord Anglesey was made Viceroy of Ireland he was put into that position with the intention of the Cabinet, and with full willingness on his own part, that a very high-handed system of authority should be established. Lord Anglesey disappointed expectation on both sides—agreeably on the part of the Catholics, and disagreeably on the part of the Orangemen. He showed himself anxious to be absolutely impartial; he tried hard to keep the Orangemen in order, and he soon came to admit the justice of the Catholic claims. William Lamb consented to become Chief Secretary to the Lord Lieutenant.

Peel then set himself down to master the Irish question. He put himself into private and continued communication with an old friend, Mr Gregory, Under-Secretary to the Lord Lieutenant, a man little disposed to favour Catholic claims; he sought information from Lord Wellesley, and of course was in regular correspondence with Lord Anglesey and Mr Lamb. One of the questions most immediately pressing for settlement was what was to be done about the Act passed in 1825 for the suppression of the Catholic Association and all unlawful societies and organisations in Ireland. This Act was aimed, of course, chiefly against the Catholic societies, but it also embraced in its scope the troublesome Orange associations. The Act, as has been said already, would expire, if not expressly continued, with the session of 1828. What was to be done? Was it to be allowed to expire? Was some other measure to be devised which should succeed it, and should do the work it had failed to do? There could be no second opinion as to the failure of the Act. The Catholic associations and the Orange societies were going on as though it had never been called into existence. The opinions of the authorities were various. Lord Anglesey wrote to William Lamb imploring him to 'keep matters quiet in Parliament, if possible,' and assuring him that the less said about Catholic and Protestant the better. Lord Anglesey appeared to be seized with a conviction that, if people could only be got to desist from talking over the Catholic question, the whole agitation would perish for lack of public notice—die of offended pride because no man regarded it. The gallant soldier was puzzled by the condition of affairs, and was well nigh at his wits' end for a mode of remedy. He was clearly, however, against the renewal of the Act of 1825. 'If,' he says, 'we have a mind to have a good blaze again, we may at once command it by re-enacting the expiring Bill; and when we have even improved it, and rendered it perfect, we shall find that it will not be acted upon.' Mr Lamb wrote to Peel to say that, if a measure could be framed which would prevent perpetual debate in Dublin upon Roman Catholic affairs, it would be a very good thing, and would be secretly approved of by all the more moderate and rational among the Catholics themselves. But he had wholesome doubts as to whether any such Act could be devised, or whether, even if it were devised, it could be applied. He falls back upon great hopes—the old, familiar hopes—that the Catholics would quarrel among themselves; he thinks they are, indeed, already beginning to quarrel among themselves, and there may be some chance of getting rid of the agitation in that way. They were perplexed in the extreme, these men of Dublin Castle, in those days. One reads the letters of Lord Anglesey with an almost unqualified admiration for the kindly and generous nature of the man, and for the positively impassioned desire of the Waterloo hero to avoid any spilling of blood. The voice of Lord Anglesey is always for moderation and for peace. He did not see his way, indeed; but, at the time, who did? He appears to have had instincts which might have guided him better than professional statesmanship appeared likely to guide other men.

Peel kept his head perfectly cool and his judgment clear and unclouded all this time. He had to keep his mind upon England and Ireland at once. While closely considering what could be done in the way of legislation to keep Ireland quiet, he had also to take account of all that was passing in England with regard to the grievance of which Ireland most bitterly complained. On May 8, 1828, a resolution was brought forward in the House of Commons by Sir Francis Burdett, declaring it expedient to consider the state of the laws affecting his Majesty's Roman Catholic subjects in Great Britain and Ireland, 'with a view to such a final and conciliatory adjustment as may be conducive to the peace and strength of the United Kingdom, to the stability of the Protestant Establishment, and to the general satisfaction and concord of all classes of his Majesty's subjects.' This resolution was carried by a majority of 272 to 266. 'There was thus,' Peel says in one of his Notes, 'for the first time in that Parliament, a majority of the House of Commons in favour of the Roman Catholic claims.' Still more significant, perhaps, is another comment made by Peel. 'It was remarked by Mr Brougham, who closed the debate, that no single member of those who had opposed the motion of Sir Francis Burdett had affirmed the proposition that things could remain as they were, and that it was impossible to conceal or deny the great progress which this question had made in Parliament and the much greater out of doors.'

That was just the consideration to give Peel pause, to make him stop and think, to make him keenly question himself—the consideration that no man—no, not one—among the sturdiest opponents of Catholic Emancipation in the House of Commons 'had affirmed the proposition that things could remain as they were.' For a man who is not a dreamer or a mere fanatic this consideration is a call to action. A constructive statesman then asks himself only as to the best course reform can take. The day for blankly opposing it is gone for him. It is interesting, too, to notice the quiet, practical way in which Peel enumerates the principal speakers on both sides of the debate. On the side of Sir Francis Burdett there are Sir James Mackintosh, William Lamb, Charles Grant (President of the Board of Trade), Huskisson, Brougham, and many others of weight and capacity. On the other side are Sir Charles Wetherell, Sir Robert Inglis, Leslie Foster, and the like. Peel dryly observes that, 'without depreciating the abilities or authority of those who concurred with me in resisting the motion'—he was one of those who voted against it—'any one acquainted with the House of Commons at that time would readily admit that the great preponderance of talent, and of influence on the future decisions of the House of Commons, was ranged on the other side.' The Government had made up their minds not to seek from Parliament a continuance of the Act of 1825.

An unexpected debate on a side issue hastened a crisis in Irish affairs, and forced the hand of Peel. There was a Bill brought into Parliament for the disfranchisement of the borough of East Retford. Huskisson was pledged to support the transference of the seat to Birmingham. The Government would not accept that policy. Huskisson voted against his colleagues, and sent a letter to the Duke of Wellington offering to resign his place in the Administration. The Duke acted as though the offer to resign were an absolute resignation, and calmly accepted it. Huskisson wrote to explain; but the Duke would not see it, and held to his resolve. Huskisson had nothing for it, of course, but to give up his office. The affair created a great sensation at the time; it was made the theme of an amusing comic song in the late Lord Lytton's novel, *Paul Clifford*, published so long after the dispute as 1830.

But, it may be impatiently asked, What has this to do with Ireland and the Catholic question? As the result will show, it had much to do with both. The friends of Huskisson greatly resented Wellington's treatment of him and the Canningite members of the Government followed up Huskisson's resignation by their own. Lord Palmerston, Lord Dudley, Charles Grant, and William Lamb resigned. Among the changes which were occasioned by this wholesale resignation of offices, was the appointment of a new President of the Board of Trade, in the room of Charles Grant. The post was offered to Mr Vesey Fitzgerald, a distinguished Irishman, who sat in the House of Commons for the county of Clare. Fitzgerald accepted the offer, and had, accordingly, to resign his seat, and seek for re-election at the hands of his constituents. Just before the dispute with Huskisson, Peel had positively made up his mind to resign his office, and become a private member. The defeat of the Government on the motion of Sir Francis Burdett had decided him to take a step which he had long been contemplating. The decision of the House in that case left him, as leader of the Government there, in a minority on what he justly describes as 'the most important of domestic questions,' and he felt that under such conditions he could not continue to lead the House which had thus virtu- ally thrown him over. But when Huskisson, Palmerston, Lamb and Grant resigned, he felt that that was not the time to withdraw his co-operation from the Duke of Wellington. He swallowed his dissatisfaction and humiliation at the result of the debate on Sir Francis Burdett's motion, and he made a loyal resolve not to withdraw from the side of his friend when his friend was in embarrassment and in difficulty. The loyalty of Sir Robert Peel to the Duke of Wellington, and his determination to remain in the Government just then, perhaps saved England from the horrors of a civil war.

When Mr Vesey Fitzgerald resigned his seat in order to seek re-election, the leaders of the Catholic Association determined to oppose him. The resolve was not without its risks. Vesey Fitzgerald was a very popular man. He had always been a supporter, by voice and vote, of the Catholic claims. His father had been one of the most resolute of those who fought by the side of Grattan, and of Sir John Parnell, against the Union. Still, he was about to become a mem- ber of a Government which was now, since the secession of the Canningites, resolutely set, to all appearance, against the Catholic claims; and the leaders of the Catholic Association determined, at all cost and risk, to oppose him. The difficulty was how to find a fitting opponent. According to the law, the opponent must be a Protestant. It was found very hard indeed—in the end it was evidently impossible—to find any suitable candidate. At last O'Connell took what then seemed the desperate resolve of disregarding the law, and standing as a candidate for Clare county himself. An influential nobleman, a consistent friend of the Catholic claims, exclaimed when he heard the news: 'This is going too far; O'Connell will end by getting himself hanged.'

The struggle that followed was one of the most remarkable in the history of modern Parliamentary elections. Perhaps it would not be saying too much if we were to call it the most remarkable. On the one side was all the influ- ence of the Government and of the class, including even the underhand influence of some of the Catholic landlords. On the other side were the peo- ple, the priests—especially the younger priests—and the gigantic power of O'Connell. It is interesting to read the letters of Vesey Fitzgerald to Peel while the contest was still in progress. Fitzgerald, although a polished gentleman and thorough man of the world, appears to have almost completely lost his head. 'The proceedings of yesterday,' he tells Peel in a letter, 'were those of madmen; but the country is mad.' More than once he writes in all the amaze- ment of a man who thinks the end of the world is coming, and is coming on his account, to vex him in particular. It would seem as if it had never occurred to him before that the vast bulk of the Irish Catholics might one time or other make some rally for their rights. He writes as a Southern planter might have written if he had found a negro slave setting up as his rival in candidature for a seat in the American House of Representatives. He is full of denunciation of O'Connell, and, among other things, declares that O'Connell does not dare to come to Clare in person—that he is 'afraid of personal risk and danger.' Of course, O'Connell went to Clare, and did not seem to know that he was in any particular danger, or to care about it. Fitzgerald wrote to Lord Anglesey despondently, and calling for a stronger military force in Clare. Lord Anglesey explains to Peel what is the strength of the military force in Clare. He speaks with the quiet, half-concealed contempt of an experienced soldier about the alarms of the Clare landlords, and adds, that if the force he had concentrated on Clare 'cannot keep one county quiet, we are in a bad way.' He adds, however, with an appreciation of the real condition which some of the statesmen did not perceive, 'I cannot persuade myself that there will be serious riot. I really believe the agitators are anxious to preserve order, and that they have the power as well as the inclination to accomplish it; it will be an additional triumph to them.' One of the most conspicuous champions and supporters of O'Connell in this Clare Election was a man whose living appearance is still familiar to those who know the House of Commons. In the various correspondences which passed between Peel and Lord Anglesey, Peel and Lord Francis Gower (who succeeded Mr Lamb in the office of Chief Secretary), few names appear more often than the name of The O'Gorman Mahon. Peel and O'Connell and Anglesey have long since passed away, and are to the present generation only figures in history; the tall and stately form of The O'Gorman Mahon, hardly even yet bowed with years, is familiar to all who visit the House of Commons in our own day.

Order was preserved during the contest, and O'Connell was elected. A great constitutional crisis had come. No living man detested Catholic Emancipation more than Lord Eldon. But Lord Eldon, with all his fierce and unconquerable prejudices, was a man of intellect, and a man who was not afraid to look realities straight in the face. He wrote to his daughter immediately after the result of the struggle in Clare had been made known: 'Nothing is talked of now which interests anybody the least in the world except the election of Mr O'Connell.' He adds: 'At all events this business must bring the Roman Catholic question, which has been so often discussed, to a crisis and a conclusion. The nature of that conclusion I do not think likely to be favourable to Protestantism.' Lord Anglesey wrote to Lord Francis Gower a letter, of which he desired that communication might be made to the Duke of Wellington and to Peel, on the subject of the Catholics and their movement, as affected by the Clare Election. In that letter he says: 'I believe their success inevitable; that no power under heaven can arrest its progress. There may be rebellion—you may put to death thousands—you may suppress it; but it will only be to put off the day of compromise.' Lord Anglesey again and again answers, to the arguments of those who are for letting things stay as they are rather than run any risk—that things will not stay as they are; that no power on earth can keep them as they are.

During the whole of this terrible crisis, when, in the judgment of many calm and sensible observers, rebellion in Ireland was certain to come, Peel never lost his composure. He looked quietly, searchingly, over the whole field of controversy. He sought information from every source. At one moment he asks himself whether it might not be possible that the fever of political and religious excitement which was quickening the pulse and fluttering the bosom of the whole Catholic population—which had inspired the serf of Clare with the resolution and the energy of a freeman—which had in the twinkling of an eye made all considerations of personal gratitude, ancient family connection, local preferences, the fear of worldly injury, the hope of worldly advantage, subordinate to the one absorbing sense of religious obligation and public duty—whether, I say, it might not be possible that the contagion of that feverish excitement might spread beyond the barriers which, under ordinary circumstances, the habits of military obedience and the strictness of military discipline oppose to all such external influences. The ranks of the Army swarmed with Irish Catholics who had done splendid service in the Peninsula. Could such men be always securely trusted to see their co-religionists engaged in a deadly struggle for equal rights of citizenship, and not feel tempted to stand by their side? Peel, a civilian, thought it very doubtful. Anglesey, a distinguished and experienced soldier, thought it more doubtful still. What could be done if the Catholics in the Army were not to be trusted to stand to their ranks?

Nothing can show the true genius of the statesman more clearly than the manner in which Peel allowed himself through all this crisis to be educated by the teaching of facts. Some of his words which we have quoted show that he had that sympathetic—what may be called that dramatic—insight which enables one to interpret the feelings and the minds of people totally unlike himself, and without which gift there can be no real statesmanship. The words in which Peel speaks of the O'Connell contest having 'in the serf of Clare with the resolution and the energy of a freeman,' are a noble evidence of

Peel's dramatic and statesmanlike faculty. To almost all around him the whole agitation was a mere political and social nuisance.

A contempt for O'Connell was a part of the faith of the Tory politician of that day. Vesey Fitzgerald described O'Connell as a person so degraded that a man of honour could not even call him to account for his calumnies. Even Lord Anglesey constantly writes of 'O'Connell and his gang.' Lord Anglesey was, indeed, in favour of Catholic Emancipation, but he 'abhorred the idea of truckling to the overbearing Catholic demagogues.' Nobody in Peel's set, but only Peel himself, seems to have had any idea that, after all, O'Connell may have been representing a great national and religious cause. 'Ireland is going mad' was the conviction of many men as well as Vesey Fitzgerald. Ireland was going mad—that was the easiest solution of the whole question. But it was not a solution to satisfy Peel. Peel was too great a statesman to believe in the temporary insanity of nations, or to found any policy on the theory that a people could be composed of two or three self-seeking scoundrels and some millions of crazy dupes. While other English statesmen were railing at the wicked leaders and the Bedlamite followers in the Irish movement, Peel was asking himself whether, after all, there might not be something strong, genuine, and deep-rooted in that feeling which, to use his own words—words that might have come from the lips of O'Connell himself—'had inspired the serf of Clare with the resolution and the energy of a freeman.'

The end could not be far off when such thoughts had begun to take possession of the mind of Robert Peel. The election of O'Connell was in itself a peaceful revolution.

VI

Catholic Emancipation Coming

Dismissal of Anglesey—Crisis in the viceroyalty—The King's obstinacy—Peel makes up his mind that Catholic Emancipation must come at once—He prevails upon Wellington

NOT MANY MEN, HOWEVER, EITHER in England or in Ireland, were yet inclined to believe that the revolution had been accomplished, or that it would be peaceful. O'Connell was, indeed, elected; but there remained the question whether he would be allowed to take his seat, and whether, if he were not allowed to take his seat, expulsion from the House of Commons would not be the signal for the outbreak of a rebellion in Ireland. The almost universal opinion among the Irish authorities was, that if O'Connell were expelled from the House there would be rebellion. Such was the conviction of the stout-hearted Anglesey himself. He was not afraid of the ultimate results, but his soul sickened at the prospect of having to drench the country with blood for the sake of keeping up a sectarian ascendency of which he disapproved, and putting down a movement of which he cordially approved. He wrote to Peel again and again, stating his views very clearly. His conviction was that there was but one way out of the trouble, and that was the emancipation of the Roman Catholics. The winter would pass over quietly—that was his great hope and comfort; and then, as he put it, will have time to legislate before we begin to light. Seize your opportunity, then—such was the effect of his urgency—legislate in the proper way, emancipate the Roman Catholics, and we shall not merely not have to fight in Ireland at all, but we shall have secured the loyal service of any number of stout Irishmen to fight with us the battles of the empire.

The advice was soldierly, manly, sensible. So far as Peel was concerned it was, however, only preaching to the converted. But Peel saw immense difficulties with which the mind of Lord Anglesey had no occasion to concern itself. First, there would be the Duke of Wellington to gain over. That Peel knew could be done. He knew well that the Duke would accept any policy which Peel could show him was necessary for the stability of the empire and for the due carrying on of the King's Government. But the King himself? How was he to be won over? What kind of argument could prevail with that narrow and obstinate mind? The King had of late been talking as strongly and as fiercely against Catholic Emancipation as he had done at any other time. Then, how to prevail over the great bulk of the Tory party, who were pledged to the lips to the doctrine of Protestant ascendency? We can well believe that Peel passed many an unquiet hour. He did not shrink from any of the consequences which might follow from the adoption of the policy which he was now all but determined to adopt. He has left us by his own hand the fullest exposition of the successive workings of his mind; of the manner in which conviction grew to take firm and firmer hold upon him. There is not in the history of statesmanship any record of a more severe internal struggle brought to an end at last by a more conscientious and self-denying resolution. Peel made up his mind to go in for Catholic Emancipation. 'Being done,' in Shakespeare's words, 'there is no pause for him.' The difficulties with which Peel had to deal may be illustrated by the fate of the Marquis of Anglesey. In the year 1828—the year at which our history has now arrived—there was a correspondence between Lord Anglesey and the Roman Catholic Primate of Ireland, in which Lord Anglesey bluntly; and somewhat incautiously, declared that he did not agree with the Duke of Wellington on the subject of Catholic Emancipation. This came to the ears of the King, and, as Peel somewhat significantly puts the matter, 'it became necessary at the close of the year to intimate to Lord Anglesey that we felt it to be our duty to advise the King to place the Government of Ireland in other hands.' The King, in fact, would have no more of Lord Anglesey; and, of course, the Duke of Wellington did not approve of a Viceroy who, for whatever motive, could make announcement, in a correspondence which was sure to get talked of, that some of the Duke's colleagues were opposed to the Duke's policy on the most important domestic question of the day. What was to be done? Wellington offered the Viceroyalty to peer after peer; nobody would have anything to do with it. The position was too precarious; the conditions were too perplexed. Each man who in turn declined the office would have accepted it willingly if the Government could make up their minds to attempt a settlement of the Catholic question. Even at the very close of the memorable year, 1828, the mind of the Government was not made up. But the mind of Robert

Peel was fully made up. He saw his way. He formed a decision of which he was fairly entitled to say 'that it was wholly at variance with that which the regard for my own personal interests or private feelings would have dictated.' Twenty years after Peel wrote the declaration that the decision he had come to in 1828 was adopted 'with a clear foresight of the penalties to which the course I resolved to take would expose me the rage of party, the rejection by the University of Oxford, the alienation of private friends, the interruption of family affections.' These are pathetic and manly words.

Peel wrote to the Duke of Wellington telling him he had made up his mind that there must be a settlement of the Catholic question, and that the settlement should be, if possible, a complete one. Peel told the Duke that he had not changed his views as to the danger of Catholic Emancipation—that he still disliked and dreaded it, but that the time had come when a choice had to be made between one danger and another, and that the danger of resisting Catholic Emancipation seemed to him now far greater than the danger of conceding it. In fact, he gave the Duke the assurance of his firm conviction that the Government ought at once to take up the subject, and bring in a complete measure of Catholic relief. But Peel was decidedly of the opinion that he himself ought to resign office, and support the Government from the outside. He was especially strong in his opinion that he ought not to be the man to introduce the measure. He foresaw the strong feelings of anger which would be aroused among the more extreme Tories when it became known that he, on whom they had relied as their chief rampart against Catholic Emancipation, had become the bridge across which the measure was to pass. He was honestly convinced that it would smooth over some difficulties for the Government if the measure were to be introduced by some man around whom so many feelings of bitterness would not centre. Then, again, there would have to be negotiations with the Catholics, there would have to be compromise, there must be give and take; and Peel thought that all such arrangements could be more satisfactorily made if the measure were in the hands of a man who had never been so deeply committed to an anti-Catholic policy as he had been during all his previous political career.

Such were the opinions which Peel laid before the Duke in the August of 1828. Before the closing days of that year, the Marquis of Anglesey had been turned out of office in Dublin, and had become intensely popular with the Irish people; whilst the Viceroyalty was for the time going a-begging; and, as the Duke of Wellington himself put it in a letter to Peel dated December 30, 1828, 'the whole question turns upon the Roman Catholic question.' There, at the very close of the year, the Prime Minister had still no policy to offer. Why did not Peel press his own policy on him? Peel did press his own policy on the Duke; but, in Peel's own words, 'the chief difficulty was with the King.' The King would not yet listen to reason. Even in January, 1829, the King would not consent that the subject should be taken into consideration by his Ministers. George had had several interviews with the Duke of Wellington in the autumn and early winter of 1828, and the very mention of the subject made him hot and angry. In the spring of 1829 the King kept on talking to Lord Eldon with great bitterness, declaring that he was miserable and wretched, and that if he were ever driven to give his assent to a Roman Catholic Relief Bill, he would go to Hanover, and return to England no more, and that the English people might, if they liked, get a Catholic King in the Duke of Clarence.

The Duke of Clarence had just been removed from the position of Lord High Admiral because of his high-handed action with regard to another officer. That fact, and the Duke of Clarence's open advocacy of the Catholic claims, suggested to the King the taunt which thus offered him as a Catholic sovereign to the English people.

The Duke of Wellington tried to get the Archbishop of Canterbury, the Bishop of London, and the Bishop of Durham to understand that the time had come when some consideration of the Catholic question was not only necessary, but even inevitable. He was in hope that, if he could get them to listen to reason, their example might have some influence over the King. The Duke had two interviews with the prelates; and the prelates considered the subject, and informed him that nothing could induce them to relax in their opposition to any measure for the relief of the Catholics.

The situation had become one of intense anxiety. The declared opinion of the King, of the House of Lords, and of the State Church, were all against Catholic Emancipation. Peel had made up his mind that it must come, and come quickly. He would not give way. He kept on pressing the Duke of Wellington with his advice. The Duke regarded Peel's advice with the utmost deference, and began to have no doubt whatever that Peel was right; but he did not see how he could move the King. At all events, the Duke was clear that he would have no chance whatever of moving either the King or the bishops if Peel did not remain in office. On this point he urged Peel so strongly that Peel consented to put aside his own personal feelings and even his private impressions with regard to the expediency of the step and to consent to remain in office. The Duke put it to him in such a light that it would have seemed like the desertion of some dear comrade in a moment of extremest danger if he had not consented to remain in the Cabinet to the last.

Why, it may be asked, did not the Duke and Peel, and their colleagues who thought with them, lay their views before the King, and at once resign their offices if the King would not listen to their advice? There were some good reasons to influence practical statesmen. Peel was very anxious to avoid any course of action which might drive George IV into some public declaration against a Catholic Relief Bill, from which he might afterwards plead that he could not in conscience recede. Peel feared that if the Duke and he pressed their advice peremptorily on the King, the King would regard it as though a pistol were put to his head, and would blaze out in some vehement vow of determination never to give way. Peel felt convinced, too, that if the Duke of Wellington could not obtain the King's consent, no other living man would have the slightest chance of obtaining it. He himself thought of Earl Grey, a statesman of the highest character, of great abilities, and always an avowed and steadfast friend of Catholic Emancipation. But Peel saw clearly that it would be utterly out of the question to suppose that the King would yield to Lord Grey, whom he personally disliked and dreaded, what he would not yield to the Duke of Wellington. There was nothing for it, that Peel could see, but for the Duke to remain at the head of the Administration for him to stand by the Duke's side, and for both to steer the best course they could. The one great object present to Peel's practical mind all through was the car-rying of a Catholic Relief Bill. There was a famous saying of O'Connell, when at the height of his success as a brilliant advocate, that a great speech was a good thing, but that the verdict was *the* thing. Peel's Parliamentary policy was always governed by a somewhat similar principle. The carrying of the measure was the thing with him. He would have been only too glad to leave to Lord Grey and the Whigs all the honour of carrying the measure, but he felt sure they could not carry it, and his one great purpose now was to have it carried.

Why was the King thus set against the relief of the Catholics? In his earlier days he had been in the constant companionship of the men who were the most earnest and energetic friends of liberty and of religious equality. Until a comparatively recent period he had been supposed to be in favour of Catholic Emancipation. Some writers have suggested that, when he broke from the Whigs on the question of the French Revolution, he broke from them on all questions that concerned the government of peoples, and religious equality became in his eyes something as odious as political democracy. But it is certain that long after that time, George, while Regent, was understood by those who came nearest to him to be still in favour of doing justice to the Catholics.

Why had he suddenly become so bitterly and angrily opposed to their claims? Lord Dalling, in his 'Historical Sketch' of Sir Robert Peel, gives it as his opinion that the change came altogether out of the dislike which George, when Regent, had begun to feel for the proud, unbending ways of Lord Grey. George had been used to adulation, to servile obedience. Even so great and so true-hearted a man as Fox could condescend to humour him and compromise for him. Lord Grey would do nothing of the kind. He would not lower the proud crest of his political integrity and consistency to gratify any prince. He was a man who would not flatter Neptune for his trident, or Jove for his power to thunder. George hated him, and soon came to include in his hatred for Lord Grey the cause of which he was the advocate, and the members of the religious denomination whom he would have emancipated. Lord Dalling's explanation is apt and of good seeming. George had a narrow, petty, selfish mind, incapable of high, impartial thought. He found that the policy of Grey was winning in spite of him, and he hated the policy all the more on that account. It is probable that there is no other explanation. We cannot suppose George IV to be suddenly seized by any passion of religious bigotry, such as that which always held genuine hold over the mind of George III.

The Duke of Wellington came to the conclusion that the only chance of carrying the policy on which Peel had now set his heart, and to which, because of him, Wellington himself had given his assent, was to obtain from the King permission to consider in the Cabinet the whole question of Ireland, including in it, of course, the question of Catholic relief. Peel drew up an elaborate Memorandum on the state of Ireland, chiefly with regard to the Catholic question, in which he set forth clearly and elaborately his reasons for believing that the time had come when the settlement of that question was inevitable. The Memorandum, which bore the date January 12, 1829, was submitted to the King by the Duke of Wellington. The day after the King had received it, those of his Ministers who had, up to that time, voted uniformly against the Catholic claims, waited separately on George, and each expressed a general approval of the opinions set out in the Memorandum. The Ministers who waited on the King were the Duke of Wellington, the Lord Chancellor (Lyndhurst), Lord Bathurst, Mr Goulburn, Mr Herries, and Peel himself. The Duke of Wellington, when once he had made up his mind to any course of action, was the very man to prevail over such a sovereign as George IV. The Duke carried into civil life the temper and the policy of the commander-in-chief. He saw what was to be done, and he was determined that everybody should do it. He had unbounded respect, veneration, homage for the office and the person of the Sovereign; but when he was put in command of the hour, he expected that the Sovereign would be guided by his directions—would obey his word of command. If George IV had really—as in his cups he used to say he had—served at Waterloo, and served under the Duke of Wellington, the Duke, with all his reverence for his future Sovereign, would have taken good care that the future Sovereign should obey the orders of the Commander in-Chief. Wellington appears to have argued it out much in this way: 'Peel knows all about it; the King does not, and I do not. Peel is the man to advise; he has told me what to do, and I am going to do it. It is for the King's own good—Peel says so, and he knows. I have got to make the King take Peel's advice, and he shall take it.'

The result of the pressure brought to bear by the Duke was that the King consented to allow the Cabinet to consider the whole state of Ireland, and submit their views to him. The King made, however, the *proviso* that he was in no degree pledged to the adoption of the views of his Government, 'even if it should concur unanimously in the course to be pursued.' In the memorandum made by Peel of the King's decision, not a word is said about the Catholic question. Probably George was induced to give his curiously-qualified consent by the consideration that he was not compelled to make specific mention of the hateful Catholic question. The English people were some lengths away from constitutional government at that time. The *proviso* of the sovereign would be as impossible in the England of our day as the sending of a bow-string to the Minister of whose advice the sovereign did not approve.

By this time the 17th of January had arrived, and Parliament was to open on the 6th of February. The interval was but short for the preparation of the measures which would have to be submitted to both Houses and, of course, it was absolutely necessary that the Speech from the Throne should contain a general indication of the policy of the Government with regard to Ireland. The construction of these measures would have to be the business of Peel, and their presentation to the House of Commons, and their advocacy there, would be in his hands. Peel determined that the measure for the relief of the Catholics should be preceded by a Bill to suppress the Catholic Association, and other such associations, in Ireland. He also determined to accompany the measure of relief by a measure to alter the elective system in Ireland, by getting rid of the forty-shilling freeholder, who had been the main support of O'Connell in Clare. Finally, he made up his mind that the Catholic relief measure must not be in any sense retrospective, and that O'Connell, although elected for Clare, must not be enabled by the Bill to take his seat without being put to the trouble of a second election. In all these determinations—except, of course, that which related to the Catholic Relief Bill—Peel seems to have made a grievous mistake. It was a mistake to precede or to accompany the measure of relief by any legislation directed against the movement without whose impulse he himself would never have acknowledged the expediency of conceding the Catholic claims. It was a mistake to mix up the measure of Catholic relief with a sort of emasculation of the Irish franchise. It was a mistake not to open the doors of the House of Commons freely, generously, and at once, to O'Connell, seeing that he had been fairly elected, and that he was perfectly certain to be elected again. The Catholic Relief Bill ought to have been granted in the most generous spirit. It was a measure of conciliation and of confidence; it ought not to have been accompanied by enactments which said to the Irish people—'You shall not do this sort of thing again'; and said to the Irish leader—'Yes, you must come into Parliament, we can't help that; but at all events we shall keep you out as long, and obstruct your entrance as much, as the literal interpretation of the law puts it in our power to do.'

VII

Catholic Emancipation Come

The King struggles and wriggles, and yields at last—Peel resigns his seat for Oxford University; stands again and is defeated—He is elected for Westbury— The Catholic Emancipation Bill passes

P EEL HAS HIMSELF GIVEN US some hints that these additional measures were not proposed out of the narrow and ungenerous spirit which they would seem to indicate. He appears to have thought that something of the kind was necessary in order to satisfy the temper of the King and the prejudices of the bishops and the House of Lords. It was necessary, also, he apparently thought, that measures should be introduced which would prove that the Cabinet had been dealing with the whole state of Ireland, and not merely with the question of Catholic Emancipation. Any affront to O'Connell, any obstacle put in the way of his entering the House of Commons, would humour the King, and gratify the Lords and the bishops, and a large number of all classes in England.

The King gave what Peel calls a reluctant assent to the proposals of the Cabinet. It was, indeed, a very reluctant assent. There was some angry controversy, and there were moments when all hope of carrying on the Government under Wellington and Peel seemed to have come to an end. But George really had no one to turn to if he were abandoned by Wellington and Peel, and at last he gave his unwilling, extorted, and ungracious assent. He submitted to Peel, and detested him for ever after. Peel now was as obnoxious to him as Lord Grey had been. To Peel, however, the House of Commons was far more than the King; the country, still more than the House of Commons. He was not cast in the mould that makes men the favourite of sovereigns. There are some fine lines in Webster's *Duchess of Malfi* which tell us—

An honest statesman to a prince
Is like a cedar planted by a spring:
The spring bathes the tree's root; the grateful tree
Rewards it with his shadow.

Such, however, were not exactly the relations which existed between George IV and the honest statesman who was his Minister.

Parliament opened on the 6th of February, 1829. The Speech from the Throne informed the Houses that the state of Ireland had been the object of his Majesty's continued solicitude. Then it went on, first to deplore the existence in Ireland of an Association which is dangerous to the public peace, and inconsistent with the spirit of the Constitution; which keeps alive discord and ill-will among his Majesty's subjects, and which must, if permitted to continue, effectually obstruct every effort permanently to improve the condition of Ireland. The King asked for powers to deal with that and other such associations, and then recommended that, when that had been done, Parliament should take into its deliberate consideration 'the whole condition of Ireland,' and should 'review the laws which impose civil disabilities on his Majesty's Roman Catholic subjects.' 'You will consider,' the Speech went on to say, 'whether the removal of those disabilities can be effected consistently with the full and permanent security of our Establishments in Church and State, with the maintenance of the Reformed religion established by law, and of the rights and privileges of the bishops and clergy of his realm, and of the Churches committed to their charge.' These institutions the King declared it to be his duty and his determination to preserve inviolate. The Bill for the suppression of the Catholic Association was soon passed into law. The measure of Catholic Emancipation would soon have to be brought forward.

Peel, meantime, felt that he was bound in conscience and honour not to continue in the representation of Oxford University without giving the University a chance of pronouncing upon his recent course of action. He had been chosen by the University as the one great champion of the Church in the House of Commons. He had been preferred to Canning on the express ground that Canning was in favour of Catholic Emancipation, while Peel was against it. Peel had now completely changed his policy, and become the leader of the movement for Catholic Emancipation. He had not changed his opinions, but he had changed his policy. It is necessary to understand this fact quite clearly if we would do justice either to Peel himself, or to those who believed that he had deserted and betrayed them. We must look the fact plainly in the face. Peel was still opposed to the principle of Catholic

Emancipation. He was a firm believer in the principle of the Protestant State Church. He did not believe the Catholics could be admitted to civil equality without danger to the position of the Protestant State Church. If he could have shaped the political conditions of the empire to suit his own convictions and wishes, he would never have proposed, or supported, or failed to oppose, Catholic Emancipation. As he had thought on that question before, so he still thought of it now that he was going to bring in a Bill to emancipate the Catholics. The difference between Peel and those who soon came to denounce him was that he was a practical statesman, and they were not practical statesmen, or statesmen of any order. Peel was in the condition of a surgeon who for a long time believes a certain perilous operation unnecessary, and refuses to authorise it; then suddenly finds that it is inevitable unless far worse danger is to be encountered; and not only sanctions the operation, but, believing he can accomplish it better than anyone else, offers to undertake the operation himself. There would be nothing inconsistent in such conduct. No one would think of saying to the surgeon: 'What an inconsistent man you are! Last week you were opposed to this operation—now you not only sanction it, but you offer to perform it yourself.'

Still, it was certain that Peel had utterly changed his policy since the time of his election as representative of Oxford, and he felt bound to give Oxford a chance of pronouncing on his conduct. He therefore resigned his seat. He was opposed by Sir Robert Inglis, an implacable Tory, and was defeated by 146 votes. A vacancy, however, occurring shortly after at Westbury, Peel offered himself as a candidate.

Sir Lawrence Peel, in the volume to which reference has been made more than once already, gives it as his opinion that Robert Peel made two mistakes in the course of his career. The first was when he resigned his seat for the University; the last will have to be dealt with later on in this volume. Why does Lawrence Peel think his great relative was wrong in resigning his seat for the University? Because, he says, it was 'a virtual concession that a member of Parliament is a delegate.' It is strange that a man of intelligence like Sir Lawrence Peel should have allowed his mind to be muddled by mere axioms and phrases. Even the precision of the Greek language would seek in vain to define the exact difference, at all times, between the duties of a delegate and a Parliamentary representative. We all feel and know that a Parliamentary representative cannot submit at all times to be a mere mouthpiece of those who send him to Parliament. There are emergencies when he must act on his own inspiration, whether he likes it or not; there are occasions when even the most modest man may feel that he understands the true interests of his constituents better, at the moment, than they do themselves. It may be his right and his duty to stand between them and some sudden impulse of passion or prejudice, some mistake arising out of ignorance or misrepresentation. But a member of Parliament must always have something of the character of a delegate. He must in general represent the opinions of those who sent him into the House, and so far he must be a delegate. Even in the days of the pocket-boroughs, the man who sat for one of these constituencies had to be sometimes the delegate of the patron who had sent him into the House of Commons. The only English member of Parliament known to fame who could claim for himself the position of one absolutely free from any of the duties of the delegate, was the member for Ludgershall, in Wiltshire, who, during the great debates on Lord Grey's Reform Bill, announced himself to the House as the owner of Ludgershall, the constituency of Ludgershall, and the member for Ludgershall, and declared that in all these three capacities he was in favour of the disfranchisement of Ludgershall. It would be absurd to suppose that any constituency could tolerate a man who, having been elected to advocate certain political principles, suddenly began to advocate the very opposite principles. It would be absurd for such a man to wrap himself up in his heroic virtue, and declare that he had suddenly been visited by an inspiration which made him much wiser than his constituents, and that he proposed to act upon that inspiration though the sky should fall. His constit-uents would begin in all sober seriousness to think that Colney Hatch rather than Westminster Palace was the proper place for a man with so absorbing a self-sufficiency. No question of personal dignity is involved, no question even of superior or inferior wisdom. It is like the case of a tutor who, being employed to teach a pupil Latin, and Latin only, persists in teaching him nothing but Greek. It is of no use the teacher protesting that he is convinced of the superiority of Greek to Latin as a language. The simple fact is that, hav-ing been engaged to teach one tongue, he has taught another. In truth, the only possible way of preventing the position of a member of Parliament from becoming that of a mere delegate, is the adoption of the course which Robert Peel so honourably adopted. Once make it known that the moment a man is elected for a constituency he is free to do exactly as he likes, without any deference to the opinions of the constituency—once set up that principle, and the English people would have to pass some Act to declare a member of Parliament a mere delegate. The unwritten law now certainly is, that when a man finds, from whatever reason, no matter how honourable and conscien-tious, he has to take some step of which his constituents greatly disapprove, he ought either to resign his seat altogether and absolutely, or he ought to resign it and, by offering himself for re-election, allow his constituents to hear his vindication of himself and pronounce upon it. This understanding, and this alone, rescues the position of a member of Parliament from being that of a mere delegate, a mere mouthpiece of the opinions of his constituents.

In Robert Peel's case these general considerations were fortified by other and more personal considerations. Peel had been elected by the University on the one especial ground that he was the champion of the ascendency of the Established Church and the opponent of Catholic Emancipation. No one can doubt for a moment that, if Canning had been also an opponent of Catholic Emancipation, he, and not Peel, would have been elected. Canning was then by far the greatest statesman and the greatest Parliamentary orator living. Peel was only beginning his career. Even if Canning had simply had an open mind as regards Catholic Emancipation, and had not freely and chivalrously committed himself to its advocacy, Peel would have had little chance against him in the University election. Peel felt all this. Peel had in some ways a nature as sensitive as Canning's own. It would be impossible for such a man to go on professing to speak for the University of Oxford, while he well knew that, on the great, burning question of the day, he was taking a course in diametrical contradiction to its judgment and its wishes. No axiom about delegates and representatives would have brought him one moment's peace of mind. In this, as in all things else, Peel looked to realities, and was not in the least governed by formulas. He saw two facts clear before him: he saw that the University had sent him into the House of Commons to oppose Catholic Emancipation, and that he now felt bound to propose Catholic Emancipation. It was not a question of axiom with him; it was a question of duty, of feeling, and of honour. He felt bound to give the University the opportunity, which was its due, of saying whether it desired that he should sit in Parliament as its representative any longer. In doing so, he not only vindicated his own honour, and did his duty to his constituents, but he took, as has been already said, the only course which can save the position of a member of Parliament from becoming that of a mere delegate.

Peel, as has been said, offered himself as a candidate for Westbury, and was elected—that is say, he was forced on Westbury by the patron of the borough; and even the patron had, according to Peel himself, considerable difficulty in compelling the place to accept him. Poor Sir Manasseh Lopes, the patron, was pelted by some of the Westbury people during the perform-ances on the hustings. Peel was returned unopposed, in the electioneering sense, for no Protestant candidate turned up in time to oppose him. Almost immediately after the official declaration of the return had been announced, a Protestant candidate in a chaise-and-four came dashing in from London. 'If he had entered the town a few hours earlier,' Peel quietly remarks 'it is highly probable that I should have fared no better at Westbury than I had done at Oxford.' The Protestant Ivanhoe had come just too late to rescue the Westbury Rebecca.

The difficulties with the King were not yet over. On Tuesday, March 3, 1829, Peel gave formal notice in the House of Commons that he would on the following Thursday (the 5th) call attention to the whole subject of the removal of the civil disabilities imposed on Roman Catholics. That evening, after Peel had given his notice, a summons came for him, the Duke of Wellington, and the Lord Chancellor, to attend the King early next day—the day just preceding that on which Peel was to make his statement. The King then announced that he could not have any alteration in the Oath of Supremacy. The three Ministers in turn explained to the King that without some alteration in the Oath of Supremacy there could be no Catholic Relief Bill, because the Oath of Supremacy contained statements which no Catholic could possibly accept. The King did not care; he would not have the Oath of Supremacy altered, would not have one jot or tittle of it altered, and would withdraw his consent to the whole Bill. The Ministers were firm. Then the King asked them all what they proposed to do. They all said that they proposed to ask for permission to announce to the two Houses of Parliament next day that they no longer held office under his Majesty. The King seemed a little taken aback, but rallied, and said he could not blame them, but he must hold to his decision. The interview lasted five hours. Then 'the King took leave of us with great composure and great kindness, gave to each of us a salute on each cheek, and accepted our resignation of office.' The picture seems a little odd to our modern notions. The battered-out old King kissing the Iron Duke, and the Chancellor, and Peel in turn, forms a group which it is impossible now to regard without a smile. No political situation could be grave enough not to make that scene seem rather ridiculous now.

The King, however, soon found that he could not form any Administration. He wrote to the Duke telling him as much, and asking the Ministers to remain in their offices and carry out their Irish policy. Peel very wisely pressed the Duke to obtain some more formal authority; and the King finally struck his colours. He gave the formal authority. The struggle was over.

The Bill passed through the House of Commons in March. It had large majorities on every division. It passed through the House of Lords in April. When introducing the Bill into the House of Commons, Peel used a fine and striking figure of speech, which was not only interesting in itself, but interesting also, almost painfully interesting, as a perfect illustration of his own attitude with regard to Catholic Emancipation. 'We cannot,' he went on to say, 'replace the Roman Catholics in the condition in which we found them when the system of relaxation and indulgence began.' 'We have removed with our own hands the seal from a vessel in which a mighty spirit was inclosed; but it will not, like the genie in the fable, return to its narrow confines, and enable us to cast it back to the obscurity from which we evoked it.'

It was not in such a tone that Burke or Canning would have spoken of Catholic Emancipation. These men would have advocated religious freedom as a good in itself, not as something to be conceded, almost with regret, when it became impossible without danger to refuse it any longer. But we have to bear in mind all through this chapter of history, that Peel did not take the same view of the subject that Burke and Canning had done. He had not the enlarged mind, any more than he had the genius, of Burke. But he was a shrewder practical statesman than Burke or than Canning, and when he had made up his mind that a certain measure ought to be carried, he bent the whole strength of his intellect, his energy, and his influence to carry it. He had that quality which Carlyle commends in Mirabeau: he 'argued not with the inexorable.' If a thing had to be done, he was for doing it at once. If he was not a Burke, neither was he an Eldon.

Peel frankly declared during the debate that the credit of settling the question belonged to others, and not to him. 'It belongs,' he said, 'in spite of my opposition, to Mr Fox, to Mr Grattan, to Mr Plunket, to the honourable gentlemen opposite, and to an illustrious and right honourable friend of mine who is now no more.' He might have added the name of Lord Grey. Bitter attacks were made on Peel for the manner in which it was alleged that he had hounded Canning—the 'illustrious and right honourable friend'—to his death, and then made use of Canning's policy. Peel replied with dignity, composure, and success: 'Whoever joined in an inhuman cry against my right honourable friend, I did not. I was on terms of the most friendly intimacy with him up to the very day of his death; and I say, with as much sincerity as the heart of man can speak that I wish he were now alive to reap the harvest which he sowed.' The charge of having hounded Canning to his death was renewed again and again at a later period in the career of Peel. It is a charge easily made, and too often made, in the case of a statesman who dies prematurely; some political rival or enemy is always said to have hounded him to his death. In truth, the Parliamentary battle is a hard fight for men of delicate constitution and sensitive nerves; it has sometimes proved too hard even for men who began with the strength of a Hercules and the nerves of an Ajax.

It broke down Walpole, and Chatham, and Pitt, and Fox. It is often a fierce, unsparing fight. In the hot struggle for principle, for party, and for passion, the men on both sides are driven remorselessly forward. It is not a time for pity and for quarter. Peel had all the genius and the joy of the strife, and he did his best against Canning, than whom few men were ever better able to defend themselves. But Peel did no more than every English leader of a party would have done. One of the men who, at a later period, made the charge most bitterly against Peel, was Disraeli. But if Peel had died at any time soon after Disraeli's philippics against him, someone would have been sure to say that Disraeli had hunted Peel to his death. It was right, however, to use the illustrious name of Canning in that debate. From whatever cause his death came so soon, he lived again in that great struggle and that great success. It was the triumph of Canning.

Soon after this, a young and promising student of the University of Oxford—William Ewart Gladstone—succeeded in carrying in the Oxford Union a vote of censure on Sir Robert Peel for the part he had taken in admitting the Roman Catholics to electoral equality. Other men, it would seem, were born Tories, as well as Peel, who were destined to be re-born into another and a more expansive political creed.

Reform

A COLLECTION OF BIOGRAPHICAL SKETCHES of statesmen belonging to the Georgian era was published in 1832. It contains a memoir of Sir Robert Peel—so far as he had then gone. It sums him up by saying that, 'as a statesman he has displayed much practical ability.' 'Uncommon industry and plain good sense,' it goes on to say, 'added to a most intimate knowledge of official business, have enabled him to master difficulties which to many politicians of more exalted intellect and greater pretensions would have been insurmountable.' The memoir winds up with the declaration that 'even those who are opposed to him in politics must admit his utility to a large extent; and no man of candour can deny that his exertions to soften the rigour of our criminal code entitle him to the gratitude of his country.' This, then, was the public opinion of Peel at the age of forty-two. Had he died just then we should have read of him, as his greatest praise, that he had much practical ability, uncommon industry, and plain good sense; that everybody admitted his utility—'to a large extent'—and that he had made honourable exertions to soften the rigour of our criminal code. To be sure, if Lord Palmerston had died at the age of sixty-five we should never have known that he was a really great Parliamentary debater. If Von Moltke had died at the age of sixty-five, we should never have known that he could direct a campaign. To modern readers, the exertions which Peel made to mitigate the rigour of our criminal code are but an episode, and an almost forgotten episode, of his career; and that he was a laborious and plodding businessman seems to us a matter so unimportant in his history as to be hardly worth mentioning. In striving to soften the harshness of our criminal code, he merely endeavoured to carry out in Acts of Parliament the humane efforts of other men. Peel never claimed to be considered as a great law reformer, although he carried great reforms in law. 'Rebellion,' says Falstaff, speaking satirically of the Earl of Worcester's excuse, 'lay in his way, and he found it.' Peel, speaking not satirically, but earnestly, and in simple good faith, might have said that law reform lay in his way, and he found it. He worked up the Jury Bill, and the Bills for the consolidation and the improvement of the criminal law, from the ideas of Mackintosh and Romilly. Why, it has been sometimes asked, did not Peel give the credit of these measures to Romilly, and Mackintosh, and such men, as he gave the credit for Catholic Emancipation to Fox, and Grattan, and Plunket, and Canning, and the credit, later in his life, of the repeal of the Corn Laws to Cobden? The answer seems clear enough. Peel never professed to do more than to adopt the ideas of Romilly and Mackintosh. To adopt them was to acknowledge them. Indeed, Peel did not go far enough for Mackintosh in his proposal to abolish the death penalty in certain cases of forgery. Mackintosh rightly desired that the death penalty should he abolished in all cases of forgery, and he ultimately carried his measure, in spite of the resistance of the Government. If any such occasion had arisen in the House of Commons as that which arose with regard to Catholic Emancipation and to the repeal of the Corn Laws, it cannot be doubted that Peel would have made as generous an acknowledgment of his indebtedness in the one case as he did in the other two. It is to Peel's great honour as a statesman that, the moment the Catholic question had been settled, and his energy was set free for other work, he turned his attention at once to various schemes of reform in our law code and in our Civil Service administration. He introduced measures by which the gallows was robbed of much of its annual prey. He had, indeed, been engaged at this work before the Catholic question came up to interrupt it; and he turned to its completion, so far as it could be completed in his day, when the Catholic question ceased to be a subject of controversy. By the Metropolitan Police Act he gave London her efficient system of police, and superseded the poor old Charleys of the days of Pelham and of Tom and Jerry. He had a genius and an omnivorous appetite for work. All the time he found leisure for the books and the pictures which he loved; he still read and re-read his favourite classic authors. He was a curious combination of the hard-working, intensely practical administrator and the *virtuoso* or *dilettante*. He must have enjoyed his life much at this time. To pass from hard, official work to a quiet read in his study, and from the quiet read in his study to the fierce, impassioned debates of the House of Commons, disciplined his nature like a healthy change of exercise. He enjoyed the vivid life of the House of Commons. Few men, indeed, have ever succeeded in that life who did not love it. One might be inclined to say off-hand that no man who did not love that life ever made a great success in it, if we did not remember the signal example of John Bright, who detested the House of Commons, and prevailed in it.

The Government emerged from the struggle on Catholic Emancipation victorious indeed, but terribly shaken. Their condition might remind one of that of the princess in the 'Arabian Nights' who fought the great battle in the cause of right against the evil genie, and who proved herself a mistress of better magic art than even his, but who won her battle with such sore trouble, and at such dire loss, that she died immediately after she had accomplished the destruction of her adversary. They had brought on themselves the deadly enmity of the old-fashioned Tories. They had not in the slightest degree conciliated the Whigs. They had not even conciliated the Irish Catholics. The manner in which Catholic Emancipation had been granted, and the manner in which O'Connell had been treated, took away from the measure much of its charm. It is probable that Peel, if left to himself—that even Wellington, if left to himself, would have ordered matters quite otherwise. Either, probably, would have taken care that, since Emancipation was to be granted, it should be granted generously, and that, as it was certain that O'Connell must come into Parliament, he should not be vainly and offensively obstructed by a futile act of postponement. The readers of the present day will fail to understand the history of that time altogether, recent and near to our own as it is, if they do not succeed in forming some idea of that sentiment of devotion to the will, the pleasure, the mere caprice of the sovereign, which was an article of faith among statesmen of all parties. It was not only Pitt who did homage to this fetish of royal will on the subject of Catholic Emancipation. We know that Fox once did homage to it as well.

The Tories therefore had a hard fight before them. No sooner had the Catholic question been disposed of than the Reform question began to raise anew its now really formidable pretensions. There was much distress in the country. Trade was dislocated in many places; business was suspended in once flourishing cities and towns. Distress brought, as it always does, political discontent. Wellington and Peel tried to strengthen themselves by drawing to their aid some Whigs who were willing to put aside for the moment their own peculiar opinions in order to carry on the government of the country in some practical and satisfactory manner. Nothing came of these attempts; nothing solid and abiding at least. England, as Disraeli said long afterwards, does not love coalitions; and in this case even a coalition was not practicable. Lord Grey and Lord John Russell could not be expected to coalesce with the

Duke of Wellington and Robert Peel. A new power had come into the House of Commons; a new factor in every political situation—O'Connell and the Irish vote. An alliance with O'Connell soon became one of the conditions of a political party which was determined to come into office and into power.

Two events occurred which precipitated conclusions. On June 26, 1830, George IV died; and a month after, the revolution of the Three Days of July broke out in Paris. King George was hardly cold in his grave, when Charles X of France arrived an exile in England. The important fact in the death of George IV was that it brought a King to the throne who was not supposed to be pledged in advance to anything in particular. William IV had not anything like the education or the natural capacity of his dead brother, George. George IV was undoubtedly a man of culture and of talent; Thackeray was entirely mistaken in his ideas as to George's lack of natural intelligence. The prince who was summed up by Burke—much to George's personal annoyance—as 'brilliant but superficial,' could not possibly have been the mere figure of inanity and idiocy that is set up by Thackeray as a likeness of George IV. But William had a reputation for honesty and straightforwardness and for a sincere although awkwardly illustrated interest in the well-being of his people. What George IV wanted was not talent but sympathy; he could only sympathize with himself. William was understood to be likely to make in his rude ungainly sort of way a kind of Patriot King. His accession to the throne gave new hopes to the Whigs. Every one remembered his recent quarrel with the Duke of Wellington, when the Duke, perfectly in the right, insisted on a course which compelled the Duke of Clarence, as William then was, to retire from the office of Lord High Admiral. But, much more than that the Whigs relied on the character which William had some how managed to acquire for sincerity and for patriotic feeling. In fact, he did prove to be much more of a constitutional Sovereign than any of the Georges had been. The Whigs began to press on their motions for reform and for retrenchment. The King retained the existing ministry, but there was a very widespread impression that there was going to be a break up before long. Then came the Revolution in France, and the modern history of England has always curiously vibrated to the sound of the great movements in France. An anti-reforming Sovereign and an anti-reforming ministry in France had gone down—who could doubt of the moral effect of such a lesson on the population of England; on the Liberal party of England? The King's speech at the meeting of the new Parliament in November 1830, contained no allusion to the necessity for any manner of Parliamentary reform. Lord Grey in the House of Lords complained of this; and his complaint drew from the Duke of Wellington a comprehensive declaration against all schemes of Parliamentary reform. The Duke would make no compromise, would hold out no hope. The speech is almost touching in its frank simplicity and its absolute conviction. We are borne back to quite another era of man's history as we read it. There is probably no English public man now living who would profess to be so certain of the perfection of any human institution whatever as the Duke of Wellington declared himself certain of the perfection of the existing constitution—that constitution which was destined to be completely reorganised within less than two years. Never, the Duke proclaimed, would he as a Minister have anything to do with any scheme which proposed to touch that ark of the covenant.

This must have been a somewhat startling announcement to Peel—now by the death of his father become Sir Robert Peel. We have the authority of Lord Dalling and Bulwer for saying that Peel 'was by no means pleased with this hasty and decided announcement.' Indeed, we hardly need any authority to make us feel well assured on this subject. Peel as a genuine and a practical statesman had a natural contempt for theories of finality, and for hard and fast lines in political affairs. He reasoned *a posteriori,* and not *a priori,* in such matters. He must have clearly foreseen the disadvantage at which the Duke's unstatesmanlike and sweeping declaration would place the Government. He could not of course contradict or correct his leader; but he went as far as he could in the House of Commons to break the force of the Duke's declaration by saying for himself that he did not 'at that moment see any prospect of such a measure of safe and moderate reform as his Majesty's Government might be inclined to sanction.' But the words of the Duke could not be recalled. 'Thus said the Duke; thus did the Duke infer.' The effect was to give an immense stimulus to the Reform party all over the country. They had a new King, supposed to be fond of popularity and in sympathy with the people. They had the lesson taught by France to encourage and enlighten them. They had the declaration of the Tory Prime Minister, that he would never under any circumstances favour any measure of Parliamentary reform. They had the evidence of the modified declaration of the leader of the Government in the House of Commons to prove that the Cabinet were not quite in union on that very question of Parliamentary reform. How could there be a more hopeful conjunction of conditions for a regular attack upon the Government?

The attack was soon made. It was led by Sir Henry Parnell (afterwards the first Lord Congleton), an ancestor of the present leader of the Irish National Party in the House of Commons. Parnell's attack, which was opened on November 14, 1830, came in the shape of a motion for a committee to take into consideration the estimates and amounts proposed for the Civil List. The Government strenuously opposed the motion, and were left the following evening in a minority

of twenty-nine. It was not a motion that would in those days have been supposed to call necessarily for a ministerial resignation; but Wellington and Peel
saw a cloud of difficulties and dangers surrounding them, and were honestly
convinced that they had no longer the confidence of the country. Nothing was
more curious than the manner in which they were opposed. Sir Henry Parnell
was, by conviction and by family traditions, a devoted supporter of the policy of
Catholic Emancipation. Yet he took the first opportunity in his power to turn
out the Ministry which had carried Catholic Emancipation, and which alone
could then have carried it. He was not to blame; he was perfectly right. We cannot found a political policy on the principle of gratitude. Parnell and his friends
had carried Catholic Emancipation through Peel and Wellington. That was
done with; and they now wanted to carry Political Reform. Wellington would
not have anything to do with such a task. The clear course for the Liberals was to
try to get some statesmen who would. To have any hesitation about this would
be as absurd as for a man to say that out of gratitude to the London and North-
Western Railway Company for bringing him from Manchester to Euston he
would decline to accept the services of the Great Western Company in carrying him from Paddington to Bristol, although he wanted to get to Bristol
and the North-Western line could not carry him thither. But the Wellington
administration was also opposed by some reformers of a peculiar order—bitter
and envenomed Tories who had turned reformers merely because Wellington
and Peel had emancipated the Roman Catholics. These men—they were not
many, but they were very active and unscrupulous—suddenly declared for
Parliamentary reform, partly because they had a wild hope that if the franchise
should be made more popular there was enough of the no-popery feeling among
Englishmen to carry a repeal of the Emancipation Act, and partly because they
thought any stick was good enough wherewith to beat the Tory statesmen who
had refused to govern England on the principle of religious disqualification.

　　Peel took the whole crisis with that magnanimous patience which was part
of his nature. He had never for a moment fancied that by passing Catholic
Emancipation he would doing anything to make his position as a statesman in office any stronger. On the contrary he knew perfectly well—he had
never attempted to disguise from himself or from others—that it must tend
inevitably, at least for the time, weaken his position. He knew very well that
the Catholic vote in Parliament would go with the party of Reform; and he
knew that he could not just then construct a party of reform out of the Tory
materials at his command. In any case the sudden declaration of the Duke of
Wellington must have brought on an immediate crisis.

The First Reform Battle

THERE WAS NO ALTERNATIVE; ABSOLUTELY none. Lord Grey had to be sent for. The King, of course, had not the same set feeling of repugnance to Lord Grey that was felt by his predecessor; indeed, on the contrary, was supposed to be willing enough to court popularity by accepting a minister who was recognised as a popular statesman. Lord Grey answered the request to form an administration with characteristic straightforwardness and resolution. His first stipulation was that electoral reform should be a Cabinet question. The condition was accepted, and Lord Grey at once formed a Ministry. He became First Lord of the Treasury; and at that time it was not so hard a task as it has since become to manage an administration with the leading statesman in the House of Lords. Lord Brougham was made Lord Chancellor—curiously enough, at the suggestion of the King. Lord Grey did not exactly know what to do with Brougham but was quite certain he could not do without him. Brougham's tremendous energy and extraordinary power of speech at the bar, at the hustings, and in Parliament, had made him the most powerful and popular man in the party. He was probably the greatest platform speaker in the country with the single exception of O'Connell. He was making money largely at the bar, and to accept any ordinary ministerial office would have been a serious sacrifice for him. He was offered the position of Attorney-General and refused it. Then the King, admonished by Lord Grey that it would be very hard indeed to get on without Brougham, suggested that the woolsack should be offered to him. It was offered, and was reluctantly accepted. To Brougham it meant loss of money, a temporary office, and the abandonment of a great popular position. It was pressed upon him, however, by Lord Grey as a duty to his party and his country; and Brougham accepted the office. His own objections were prophetic. From the hour when he took his seat on the woolsack he ceased to be a real influence in political life.

Lord Althorp was Chancellor of the Exchequer and leader of the House of Commons in the new administration. Lord Melbourne had charge of the Home Office. Lord Palmerston began his long career as Foreign Secretary. The sinecure office of the Privy Seal was given to Lord Grey's son-in-law, the strenuous and high-minded, but very hot-tempered, Lord Durham; the man who was afterwards to rescue Canada from chaos and lay the foundations of the Dominion. Lord John Russell was made Paymaster General of the Forces—a post which had been occupied by the elder Pitt and by Burke—and in his case, as in theirs, without a seat in the Cabinet. Lord Grey at once announced his intention of bringing forward a measure of Reform. He entrusted the framing of the scheme to a committee of four men—Lord John Russell, Lord Durham, Sir James Graham, and Lord Duncannon. The task of shaping a draft of the measure was deputed to Lord John Russell, and his scheme, with some modifications suggested by Lord Durham, was adopted as the plan of the measure.

This book is not intended as a history of the Reform Bill. It only concerns itself with the history of the Bill so far as it affected the career of Sir Robert Peel. There can be very little doubt that Peel, if he had had his own way and had not been stopped by the peremptory declaration of the Duke of Wellington, would have endeavoured to bring in some sort of reform scheme of his own. It would, no doubt, have been very cautious and tentative; but it is quite possible that he might have seen his way to a measure which the country could have accepted as an instalment, and that he might thus have kept his party in office for some time longer. It is even possible that if he had put his hand to the work he might have seen his way to some wider measure of redress. We have seen how, from the moment when he made up his mind to undertake a settlement of the Catholic question, he made up his mind also that it must be a real and a permanent settlement. It is quite possible that if he had once given his mind to the preparation of a Reform Bill, he might soon have come to see that the measure must rest secure on a broad basis and not be perched precariously on a narrow ledge. The impetuosity of the Duke of Wellington cut Peel off from any chance of attempting a settlement of the Reform question, and the scheme brought forward by Lord John Russell seemed to all Tory minds so sweeping and even so revolutionary in its character that it became a part of Peel's natural instincts and temper and training to oppose it to the uttermost. The Bill does not seem to us now a very audacious measure. It did nothing more than extinguish some rotten boroughs, efface the names of constituencies which were only constituencies in name, enfranchise some of the great towns, fix a regular and equal franchise in the boroughs, and modify, by some slight new introductions, the high franchise in the counties. It was not by any means a democratic measure, for it actually abolished some of the 'fancy franchises,' as we might call them, adopting the phraseology of a later day, which gave a chance here and there to the working-class. What the Bill did was to transfer the power from the upper to the middle class; from the noble to the *bourgeois*. The *prolétaire* was left completely out in the cold. The privileges he had already enjoyed were taken away from him.

Still, it cannot be denied that the Bill at the time was looked on by all the Tory party and even by some of the timid Whigs as a mere crude measure of revolution. Lord Dalling says that Lord John Russell's explanation of the Bill 'almost appeared a joke,' and insists that had Sir Robert Peel risen when Lord John sat down, and said that he would have been prepared to consider any reasonable or practical plan, but that the plan of the Government was a mockery repugnant to the good sense of the House, and that he could not therefore allow the time of Parliament to be lost by discussing it; moving at the same time the order of the day, and pledging himself to bring the question in a practical form under the attention of the House of Commons at an early opportunity, he would have had a majority of at least a hundred in his favour.'

This is rather too much of a conjecture. Even if it were well-founded, it would have made no great difference to the cause of Reform in the end. Lord Dalling is speaking only of the House of Commons; and is thinking only of that House of Commons. The whole mass of the people outside the House of Commons and all Parliamentary circles were determined that the suffrage must be extended and the electoral system reformed. But there can be no doubt that in the House of Commons itself the propositions of the Government seemed nothing short of revolutionary, and the general expectation was that the Ministry would almost instantaneously fall.

The first reading of the Bill was allowed to pass, without a division, according to the usual, although by no means the invariable, practice of the House of Commons. But with the second reading the battle set in, and the second reading was only carried by a majority of one—302 to 301. This naturally put the Opposition into the highest good spirits. It did not seem possible that a measure which had so nearly been overthrown in the open battle on the second reading could come out with life from the intricacies and ambushes and surprises of a fight in Committee. The Bill was not, however, destined to get into Committee. On the motion for going into Committee an amendment was moved which struck at one main principle of the measure, and on that amendment the Government were defeated by a majority of eight. It only remained now to dissolve Parliament and appeal to the country at a general election. The King was strongly opposed to such a step. He complained bitterly of being advised to dissolve a Parliament which had only just been elected. Grey and Brougham were firm and William IV gave way. Parliament was to be dissolved and dissolved on the Reform question.

Sir Robert Peel took a strenuous and a consistent part in opposing the Bill. It was a consistent part because although he might have been willing under favourable conditions to support or even to introduce a scheme of Parliamentary reform, yet it is certain that he would not have introduced such a scheme as that of Lord John Russell, and that he, like others, was perfectly thunder-stricken when he heard Lord John Russell's exposition of the measure. It would be hard for us now to understand how sweeping, how audacious, the Bill was considered to be by all the Tory and some of the Whig politicians. Joseph Hume declared that, radical reform as he was, the plan much exceeded his expectations, and that, with all his disposition to put confidence in ministers, he was not prepared to find them coming forward with so manly a measure. The Bill was accepted by the extreme Radical and demagogue 'Orator Hunt,' and by O'Connell, whose opinions might fairly be described as those of advanced Liberalism.

It was natural, therefore, that a man like Peel should be sincerely alarmed at such a measure and should feel, as he did, a strong and sometimes even an impassioned determination to oppose it to the last. On the second reading of the Bill, Peel spoke up strongly for the fancy franchises and for the small constituencies. One passage in his speech on this part of the subject has a personal and almost a touching interest. He spoke of 'a community, whose numbers were by the returns of 1821 not more than four thousand, and against whom this Bill had been brought without any allegation of necessity or without any case being made out against them ... I know that they have never abused their right—that the humblest man among them never obtained or asked a bribe for a vote he gave. They received me when I had been subjected to the indignity of expulsion for what I conceived to be an act of special duty, even to the Church of which I am a humble member. They returned me then as their representative, and till the necessity of the measure is established by more cogent arguments than I have yet heard, I will not consent to deprive them of their right.' The most ingenious part of the speech was the argument for the fancy franchises. Peel contended that these franchises enabled every class in the community 'in some way or other to have a voice in the election of Members of this House.' 'Now, I do not mean to say by this,' Peel interposed with characteristic caution, 'that the franchise should be extended to all the members of all the classes of the community, but that the constitution works well for having here and there an entrance channel for the broadest principle of popular representation.' Undoubtedly, Peel touched the one great error of the Bill. It did by the abolition of these peculiar franchises cut off the working classes altogether from any chance of having a vote. In some communities—that of Preston, in Lancashire, for example—there was an ancient and peculiar system of franchise which amounted to something very like universal suffrage. This was, indeed, an exceptional case, but there were many places and many franchises which admitted a working man to the electoral body. The Bill of Lord John Russell abolished all these franchises, rubbed them out, and made the system symmetrical indeed, but symmetrical at the expense of the working classes. The working classes, by whose aid mainly the Bill was carried, resented this bitterly afterwards, and it helped much to spread the growth of Chartism. Peel's argument in favour of the small and what we may call the patron-owned constituencies was ingenious. It was the argument with which we have been so familiar since his time—that these small constituencies frequently provided a haven of refuge for great and patriotic men whom some popular constituency had dismissed from its representation. Undoubtedly such things did happen. But it has to be remembered that the representation in the great constituencies was then on so narrow a basis that the declaration of a constituency was often little more than the decision of some one particular 'interest,' or clique, and that it was but the case of a man condemned by an 'interest' and rescued by a patron. Since the extension of the suffrage, we cannot remember any case in which a really able and patriotic man was left out for any considerable time—any time worth taking into account—if he desired to enter or to re-enter the House of Commons.

Peel's speech naturally contained many warnings against the spread of the democratic spirit—much denunciation of democracy. It closed with a powerful appeal to the House of Commons to take care that it did not 'signalise your own destruction by bowing down the pillars of the edifice of your liberty, which with all its imperfections still contains the noblest society of freemen known to the habitable world.' Among all the great speeches delivered in that remarkable debate, where Russell and Palmerston and Macaulay and O'Connell took part, none was more ingenious or more eloquent than that of Peel. Peel was wrong in most of his conclusions, and almost all his prognostications of danger came out to be unfounded. But this only means that he was still suffused with the old-fashioned Tory spirit; and we have to remember that his objections to Parliamentary reform in the radical sense were objections which had been shared in by Canning up to the time of his death.

An extraordinary scene took place in the House of Commons just before the dissolution. A debate was going on which turned more or less irregularly on the question of Reform, and on the impending dissolution. Suddenly the first cannon proclaiming the approach of the King was heard. Peel had just sprung to his feet and was denouncing the Reform scheme with all his energy and passion. For the first, although not the only time in his political career, he allowed himself to be utterly carried away by anger. He declaimed and stormed with all the vehemence of Brougham himself. The man habitually so cool, so cold, so self-contained, now shouted with the fury of an angry demagogue. He declared that if the Bill and the whole Bill were to be passed, 'there will be established one of the worst despotisms that ever existed.' 'We shall have a Parliament of mob demagogues—not a Parliament of wise and prudent men.' 'Such a Parliament,' he cried, 'and the spirit of journalism, to use a foreign phrase, has brought many happy countries to the brink of destruction.' He then turned on to the Ministers themselves and declared that they had shown 'during their short reign of power more incapacity, more unfitness for office, more ignorance of their duties, than was ever exhibited by any set of men who have at any time been called on to rule the proud destinies of their country.' It is curious to remember who these incapables and ignoramuses were. They were Lord Grey, Lord Brougham, Lord Althorp, Lord John Russell, Lord Durham, Lord Melbourne, Lord Palmerston, Lord Plunket, Sir James Graham, and the late Lord Derby, then Mr Stanley.

If Peel had calmly compared the intellectual power of the two sides of the debate as he did in the debate on Sir Francis Burdett's motion in favour of Catholic Emancipation, he might have spared himself a mistake in his political career, and a most unwonted and unnecessary display of passion. Eighteen years after Peel was in the House of Commons when the news came in of the Revolution in France, and the flight of Louis Philippe. Among the first who received the tidings was Mr Joseph Hume, and Hume hastened to Peel and told him what had happened. Peel's comment was significant; and it was just. That, he said, is what comes of trying to govern a country on too narrow a basis of representation. Peel now, at the time of this scene we describe, was endeavouring with all the force of his eloquence and his passion to make out that the one great danger to a state was the endeavour to broaden its basis of representation. Peel was a man to learn much in eighteen years. For the moment, however, he stood there storming against expanded representation, declaring that the policy of the Reform Ministry had even already made it no longer 'an object of fair ambition' for 'any man of equal and consistent mind to enter into the service of the Crown.' The scene was turbulent, and while Peel was still thundering forth, amid one crowd of members, madly cheering, and another crowd madly groaning and shouting, Black Rod knocked at the door to summon the Commons to the bar of the House of Lords to hear the prorogation of Parliament. Peel, all unconscious, kept on declaiming; the House kept on shouting. Black Rod knocked again and again. Then at last the Speaker and the House understood what was happening; Peel was cut off in the middle of his speech, the Speaker and the Commons rushed across the lobby to the House of Lords, and the Parliament was at an end.

X

The Battle Over

The General Elections strengthen the Reformers—The new Bill—Peel leads obstruction—The House of Lords throw out the Bill—Great popular excitement—The Lords at last have to give way and the Bill passes

'THE BILL, THE WHOLE BILL, and nothing but the Bill' was now the cry of the country. The wildest excitement prevailed. The general elections were fought, and were won by the Reformers. The Reformers were now in an overwhelming majority. The Bill was reintroduced—at least the second Bill was only a slight modification of the first. Then the opponents of the measure changed their tactics. They went in for delay and for obstruction. The policy of Parliamentary obstruction, of which we have heard so much in later days, was carried out with splendid audacity then. When the House got into Committee and began to consider the separate case of each small borough which it was proposed to disfranchise, the opportunities for obstruction became almost unlimited. Peel threw himself energetically into this obstructive policy. There was an organised system of obstruction. There was a regular division of labour which was adjusted and carried out under the directions of a committee of which Peel himself was the chairman. Between the 12th and the 27th of July, Sir Charles Wetherell spoke fifty-eight times, John Wilson Croker spoke fifty-seven times, and Peel himself spoke forty-eight times. Mr Molesworth has been at the pains in his excellent 'History of England from 1830 to 1874' to compile a list of the obstructive motions and divisions which took place in one night of these extraordinary debates. The record is amusing to read. It consists of nothing but a series of motions that the debate be now adjourned—that the House do now adjourn—that the Speaker do now leave the chair. There were no rules of procedure then to limit the right of debate on every motion of the kind, and the House had therefore to submit to an almost unending repetition of the same formal motions and the same arguments in their support.

The Bill, however, passed through the House of Commons at last. Its passing was expedited by the firm conduct of the Government, who declared that they were not to be obstructed out of their policy, and that they would, if necessary, keep the House of Commons sitting until the coming Christmas, or the Christmas following, if it were necessary, in order to have the decision of the House on the Bill. In the grey dawn of the morning of September 22, 1831, the last division was taken in the House of Commons—the division after that on the third reading—the division on the formal question 'that this Bill do now pass.' There were for the motion 345, against it 239. The majority in favour of the passing of the Bill was 100. Times had changed indeed with the House of Commons since the not distant day when Lord John Russell introduced the first Reform Bill.

We may cut short the rest of the struggle, all the more readily because Peel had little to do with it. The Bill went up to the Lords. The Lords threw it out on the motion for its second reading. There was an end of the measure for that year. The whole country was instantly aflame with passion. There were riots everywhere. The castles of great nobles were attacked and burnt down. The houses of country landlords who had opposed the Bill were laid in ruins. Bristol and other cities were like places captured after a siege. The winter was made hideous by the executions of the unfortunate and misguided men who had taken a leading part in these various disturbances. It will never be known for certain how near England came to revolution in these trying days. Parliament met again in December 1831, and Lord John Russell introduced his Bill—it was practically the same Bill—for the third time. After much opposition and obstruction, the Bill passed its third reading on March 23, 1832, by a majority of 116. Then it went to the Lords, and the great question now in the country was, What will the Lords do with it? The Lords soon made it certain what they meant to do with it. The Duke of Wellington announced that his hostility to the proposed reform was as uncompromising as ever. The Duke, with characteristic indiscretion—characteristic, that is to say, where questions of reform were involved—announced that he did not believe the King was in favour of the Bill. The bare suggestion threatened to make the King unpopular with the mass of the people all over the country. There was only one way by which to meet the determination of the majority in the House of Lords, and that was by the King's giving his consent to the creation of a number of new peers in order to overbear and to swamp the anti-reformers. It was well known that it would not be necessary to create the new peers. It would be enough that the King should give his consent to their creation in case of necessity. The necessity would not arise. In the Western wilds of America, if two enemies meet and the one has the other covered by his revolver in the first instance, the man so covered does not attempt to draw his weapon. It would be of no use. He would be shot before he could put his hand upon it, and he has to come to terms. It would have been so with the House of Lords. If the new peers were to be created they would carry the Bill. What would be the use of compelling the new creation? A small group of peers, who were styled the Waverers, had the decision in their hands. They held the balance of power. They oscillated now this way, now that way, between the Ministry and the Opposition. They were not opposed to all reform, but they did not like the Government measure, hoped to get it very much weakened, and therefore at present assisted the Tories. The King was with them in his heart. He hoped they would persevere in their action, and so compel Lord Grey to modify his terms. The Waverers were, no doubt, quite aware of the King's desires. It was certain that if the King consented to the making of the new peers, the Waverers would at once withdraw from their attitude of hostility to the Bill. But the King at first would not consent. He gave a point-blank refusal. Lord Grey instantly tendered his resignation. The King accepted the resignation, and the country seemed to be suddenly brought within measurable distance of civil war.

The King sent, by Lord Lyndhurst's advice, for the Duke of Wellington, and invited him to form an administration. The Duke, for all his courage and devotion, did not see his way, and recommended that Peel should be asked to try his hand at the formation of a Government. Peel acted with firmness and dignity. He declared that he saw no possibility whatever of his being able to form an administration which could hold up its head for a moment, and to this announcement he resolutely and very properly adhered. Then the puzzled Duke was urged to try again, and out of sheer devotion and personal loyalty to the Sovereign he did try again, and he utterly failed. The attempt died in its birth. The cry that came up from London and all parts of the provinces was appalling. The King's carriage was mobbed whenever it was seen in the streets of the metropolis. At last William had to give way. He sent for Lord Grey; he consented—most reluctantly, and with very bad grace—to the demand for the creation of the new peers; the Waverers thus covered at once gave way; there was bitter grumbling in the House of Lords, but the Reform Bill passed into law. With the King's final assent to the request of his ministers closed a long chapter of our constitutional history. That was the last time when a struggle took place between the personal predilections of an

English sovereign and the advice of his constitutional ministers. The whole crisis accomplished two objects as well as the passing of the Reform Bill. It practically defined the limits of the power of the Sovereign, and the limits of the power of the House of Lords.

The part which Peel had played throughout the whole struggle—if we except the one little outburst of somewhat undignified, and certainly very unusual, ill-temper which has been described a few pages back—was consistent, and was worthy of his character and career. He was not even then opposed to every possible scheme of reform; but he honestly regarded Lord John Russell's scheme as something which the country ought not to accept. He fought determinedly and conscientiously against it. But he fought fairly. Mr Molesworth admits that Peel's Opposition was 'much more candid and less vexatious than that of most of those with whom he was associated.' Peel fought his battle, no doubt, by obstruction; but obstruction was then, and for long years after, a recognised weapon of Parliamentary warfare. The writer of this volume has still a strong doubt whether it is well that a Parliamentary assembly should be too carefully protected against a method of Opposition which practically and avowedly aims at delaying a certain course of legislation until the attention of the whole country shall be forcibly drawn to what the Parliamentary assembly is doing. All Parliamentary systems must put up with a good deal of anomaly; and it is not always satisfactory for the best government of the country that a ruling party should be convinced it has the better of the argument, and has also had enough of it, and that it has a majority at its back to better the better argument. The consistency of Peel's conduct is shown in the fact that he made clear to all his own growing Conviction that reform of some kind was inevitable. We cannot know what inconvenience might not have arisen if, backed by the King's support, he had attempted to form an administration when the Duke of Wellington endeavoured to get him to venture on the enterprise. The Tories had the utmost confidence in his judgment and his leadership. They felt no such confidence in the political leadership of the Duke of Wellington. If Peel had believed that any good could be gained by further resistance, they would have followed him as far under fire as he chose to lead them. Another man might well have believed, or at least have hoped, that with the support of the King he could yet beat back the advance of the extreme reformers. Another man might have had the levity, and the hardihood to make the attempt. The result might have been political convulsion. It cannot be doubted that some of the great Liberal leaders were already asking themselves what course they should have to take in the event of the

King still resisting the demands of the people, and the country breaking into civil war. Is it too much to say that in such a struggle the King's crown might have gone down? Hardly too much to say that. Is it too much to say that if another Tory administration had been formed with the object of dragooning the country into submission to the abandonment of reform, the collision might have been instantly provoked? It certainly is not too much to say that. On the other hand, is it not certain that if Peel had taken office and tried to palm off on the country an emasculated and dwarfed Reform Bill, the popular anger would have been just as great as if he were to bring in no scheme of reform? It was then a grave crisis in the history of the movement when the Duke of Wellington advised that Peel should be asked to form an Administration, and the King acted on the advice. Peel was never deceived for one moment. He saw into the realities of the situation. He had a marvellous power of distinguishing between the things that he would have and the things that he could have, which, strange as it may appear at first, is one of the rarest gifts of statesmanship. He used his clear distinguishing power well on this great occasion. When he refused to form a Ministry, the Reform struggle was really at an end. The wildest Tory did not believe that there was more than one man who could stem the tide, and that man refused to make the idle attempt

XI

In and Out

The Irish Church Question—Lord Stanley leaves the Whigs—Lord Grey retires from public life—Lord Melbourne Prime Minister—The King dismisses Melbourne and Peel is called back from Rome—Again Prime Minister, and again defeated

PEEL NOW SETTLED DOWN TO the work of a leader of Opposition in the House of Commons. He accepted the Reform Act and the new system. He knew perfectly well that there was no going back on such a course as that. But he set himself to watch, with unfailing scrutiny, the measures which the Reform Ministry were about to bring in. He had come into the reformed Parliament as member for Tamworth. Among the new men of the new Parliament was Mr William Ewart Gladstone, whom we have seen, not very long before, engaged in carrying a vote of censure at the Oxford Union against the Government of the Duke of Wellington and Robert Peel because they had not stuck to the Tory colours and resisted the passing of the measure for Catholic Emancipation.

Peel felt well convinced that the Reform Ministry would do their best to deserve their title. He looked for all manner of wild projects of political and social reformation. His idea and his policy were to watch these measures, and, prevent them from being made too wide and wild and sweeping. He was resolved to give up absolutely the old Tory policy of resistance to every proposed change. He had never had much intellectual sympathy with such a policy, and now he saw that its game was quite played out, if, indeed, it had ever been able to play much of a game for long. He saw that its time was quite gone by now. He aimed at forming what might be called a Conservative party—a party which should resist sudden and uncalled-for change, but should adopt as its leading principle the recognition of the fact that change is one of the necessary conditions of a people's prosperity. The Duke of Wellington fell in with Peel's ideas—took the time, in fact, from Peel.

A season of energetic reform followed the passing of the Bill of Lord Grey and Lord John Russell. Peel supported, although in a cautious way, the efforts of the Government for the abolition of the slave system in our West Indian Colonies. O'Connell was the most uncompromising of all the opponents of slavery, refusing on one occasion to submit to a compromise which Mr Buxton himself had been prevailed upon to accept. The measure for the abolition of slavery was finally carried through, and will ever remain one of the standing glories of the British Empire. There was much trouble about legislation for Ireland, about a Coercion Bill for Ireland, about Irish tithes, and about the Irish Church. The debate on the question relating to the Irish Church proved memorable in the history of the cabinet, and, indeed, in the history of the country. Mr Ward, at that time considered a very rising member of the House of Commons, brought forward a motion declaring that the Protestant Establishment in Ireland exceeded the spiritual wants of the Protestant population, and that, 'it being the sight of the State to regulate the distribution of Church property in such a manner as Parliament might determine, it is the opinion of the House that the temporal possessions of the Church of Ireland as now established ought to be reduced.' This motion, which was commonly believed to have been inspired by Lord Durham, was seconded by Mr Grote, the famous historian of Greece. It came like the bursting of a shell in the ranks of the Administration. It involved the whole principle of existence for such an Establishment as the State Church of Ireland. Those who advocated the maintenance on principle of the Irish State Church could not possibly admit that its claim to support rested in any degree on the number of its votaries. They might, indeed, have argued with perfect justice, from their point of view, that, the fewer votaries it had, the greater was the necessity for maintaining it, and for enabling it to assume a wider spiritual activity. Those, on the other hand, who maintained that the revenues of the Church ought to he cut down to the proportion of her conversions or the numbers of her worshippers, were only preparing for the coming of the day when Parliament would say that the Establishment, as such, could give no reason for its existence at all.

The Whig party was already showing distinct lines of cleavage. It was dividing itself into Whigs and Radicals. Nor was that all: a number of the Whigs who had worked cordially with the Radicals for the passing of the Reform Bill were now showing not merely an inclination to draw bridle, but even to fall back into the Conservative ranks. It was known that

Lord Brougham was trying to arrange a compromise, by virtue of which a Commission should be appointed to inquire into the revenues of the Irish Church, and their proportion to the numbers of the population of Ireland. The immediate effect of all this was that Lord Stanley, Sir James Graham, the Duke of Richmond, and the Earl of Ripon, left Lord Grey's Administration. Lord Stanley passed away forever from the Whig party. To a more recent Parliament he was known only as an impetuous, brilliant mouthpiece of Toryism. Men of a younger generation could hardly be brought to believe that the Lord Derby who talked of his own Government Reform scheme in 1867 as a leap in the dark, was the Lord Stanley who, thirty-five years before that time, had leaped on the table at Brooks's to harangue his listeners into enthusiasm for Lord Grey's Reform Bill.

Lord Stanley had argued, in the debate on Ward's motion, firmly and broadly for the Church in Ireland as a matter of principle, political and religious. Sir Robert Peel was not prepared to go so directly into the question. He did not take high ground, it must be owned. How unsafe he felt himself to be will be seen from the fact that, in great part of his speech, he fell back upon the old argument that the Catholics had pledged themselves at the time of Emancipation that they would not ask for any measure to affect the Established Church. The argument was feeble in every way. No such compact could possibly hold good; one generation of Catholics could not bind another. More than that; no pledge given by any number of Catholics could bind the Protestants of England, or could bind the House of Commons. Nothing said by Grattan in the name of the Irish Catholics could bind Ward and Grote, who were not Catholics, or prevent the House of Commons from doing what it believed to be an act of justice. Peel professed himself quite willing to consider the expediency and the feasibility of redistributing the revenues of the Irish Church. He spoke on this part of the subject like a practical statesman. So far did he go along the way to compromise, that some of his opponents declared that he ought to have accepted the office in the Whig Government which had just been left vacant by the resignation of Lord Stanley. It was a curious case of crossing on the way: the fiery Whig had become a Tory; the born Tory was accepting one of the fundamental principles of the Whigs. The one was a statesman, the other was not. Peel's eloquence was but the instrument of his intellect; Stanley's whole intellect ran into his eloquence.

The Government defeated Ward's motion by the favourite device of the time for getting rid of inconvenient declarations of principle—the appointment of a Commission to inquire into the general subject. The whole controversy has been finally settled so long ago, that our only interest in it now is as regards the manner in which it affected the statesmen and the parties of that day. The King was very angry with the Ministers for having gone even as far as they did in the way of disestablishment; although, of course, no one then dreamed of disestablishing the Irish Church. He bore the grudge in his mind. Another dispute arose in the Government about an Irish question. A Coercion Bill had been brought in. Lord Althorp was disposed to enter into a compromise with O'Connell, and modify the measure. Lord Grey would not hear of compromise. The two statesmen resigned office; but Lord Althorp instantly came back, and Lord Grey remained out. Lord Grey was sick of the worry of official life—indeed, of public life altogether. Recent publications have shown that he was far less strong a man than we had long believed him to be: that he had some almost romantic weaknesses of character; that he could be played upon by skilful hands. It is probable that his was for the most part but a reflected greatness; the shining on him and through him of the light of that constellation of genius, eloquence, and statesmanship amid which he had moved so long. He disappears from this history. He did not live long after his retirement; we shall not see him any more.

The Ministry was reorganised, with Lord Melbourne, whom we have already known as William Lamb, for its head. Lord Althorp remained Chancellor of the Exchequer and leader of the House of Commons. Lord Melbourne had not much of the temper of the reformer in him. He was an indolent man, with some talents, with a potentiality of statesmanship in him which energy might have realised, and with a not inconsiderable critical faculty; his judgment in most matters more likely to be right than wrong. The King had long had a grudge against the Whig Ministers for what he considered their falling away on the Church question, and he suddenly and publicly unbosomed himself of his grievance in a public declaration. It was on the occasion of a birthday address delivered to him by a deputation of Irish prelates that William IV poured forth his soul. He declared, in the most impassioned manner, and with tears running down his cheeks, that, come what would, he was resolved to stand by the Church. This oration was nothing short of a public censure on his Whig Ministers. Everybody felt sure that something must come of it; and the something came very soon. Lord Althorp's father died; Lord Althorp thereupon became Earl Spencer, and was removed to the upper House. Some administrative rearrangements were made necessary by this change, and when Lord Melbourne went to the King to talk over them, William bluntly informed him that he did not propose to go on with his present advisers and that he had sent for the Duke of Wellington. Lord Melbourne was honestly delighted to be out of the whole affair. The strength of the Administration, such as it was, mainly depended on the influence of Lord Althorp over the House of Commons. The condition of things would be very different indeed with Lord Althorp in the House of Lords. The King himself gladly seized on this fact as another reason for getting rid of his Whig advisers.

This was indeed a crisis. The King's final communication to Lord Melbourne was dated 'Pavilion, Brighton, November 14, 1834.'

Sir Robert Peel had left England for Rome exactly a month before the date of the King's letter. The Duke of Wellington strongly advised the King not to think of any Prime Minister but some statesman who should be in the House of Commons. Of course, he advised the King to invite Peel to form an Administration, and he offered, if it would make matters more easy, in the meanwhile to hold the offices of First Lord of the Treasury and Home Secretary until Peel should return to form a Ministry for himself. Nothing could be more unfair, the Duke said, than to call upon Peel to put himself at the head of a Government which another individual should have formed. So a messenger was sent in hot haste to Rome, to bear his Majesty's command for Peel's instant return to London.

Peel had left England with his wife and his daughter 'little foreseeing the probability of my sudden recall on any ground similar to that on which it took place, and having had no communication previous to my departure with the Duke of Wellington or any other person respecting the position and pros-pects of the Administration which existed at the time of my departure.' On the night of Tuesday, November 25, Peel and his wife and daughter had just returned from a ball at the Duchess of Torlonia's, in Rome, when the letters were put into his hands which summoned him back to England to be Prime Minister. He had already seen in the newspapers the account of the death of Lord Althorp's father; but, although he assumed as a matter of course that the event would render necessary some alteration in the arrangements of the Government, he did not expect that it would lead to the practical dismissal of the Whig Ministry. He was just about to leave for Naples, and had made all the arrangements for the journey there, and back to Rome. Of course, all these plans were now knocked to pieces, and Peel sent off a letter in which he 'begged most respectfully to assure your Majesty that he will proceed on his journey to England without a moment's delay.'

Sir Robert Peel's journey home may well inspire the man of our times with a new shrug of complacency over the improved conditions of modern civi-lisation. Of course, the whole distance between Rome and Calais had to be traversed by carriage. Sir Robert Peel, in fact, travelled from Rome to London in exactly the same way as Constantine had travelled from York to Rome some fifteen hundred years before. All that horses and sails could do for Peel, sent for to become Prime Minister of England, was done for Constantine, sent for to be Emperor at Rome; and nothing more could be done for Peel than was done for Constantine. Peel had to take the precaution of providing himself with a special and separate passport, so that, in case his wife should be unable to stand the fatigue of the continuous travel, he might be in a position to pursue his journey alone. We find it very hard now to bring home to our minds the idea of a great English statesman having to provide against the possibility of his being stopped in a journey over the Continent because of his having taken passports for himself and his wife together, and his wife being unable to accompany him in his unbroken travel. The pair began their journey at Rome about three o'clock on the 26th of November. They arrived at Dover on the evening of the 8th of December. They had travelled eight nights out of the twelve, and halted the other four only because they were not able to get on. It may interest modern readers, who are acquainted with the comforts of the *train de luxe* and the 'club train' to Italy, to know what were the causes which made it necessary for Peel to submit to these stoppages on his way. One night was spent at Massa, because the way was barred by a rapid torrent which could not be ferried over in the dark; one night at Susa, as the crossing of Mont Cenis could not be begun until daybreak; one night at Lyons, which had just been declared in a state of siege, and where the travellers had to remain until all manner of formalities about their passports had been gone through; and, finally, one night in Paris, where they were expecting letters which it was necessary they should get before going on to London. Peel made the best of everything, and observes in his *Memoirs* that the long journey had the advantage of giving him ample time for considering his future action 'coolly and without interruption.' He arrived in London very early on the morning of December 9, having travelled all night from Dover; and he at once presented himself to the King. He told William straight away that he had no hesitation in undertaking to form an Administration.

Peel was acting simply in obedience to a characteristic and a dominant sense of duty. He felt that he could not leave the King in a position of difficulty. He felt that he could not leave the King 'to the humiliation, through my refusal of office, of inviting his dismissed servants to resume their appointments.' But he had little taste for the work just then. To begin with, he did not approve of the manner in which the late Ministers had been dismissed. He did not think Lord Althorp's removal to the House of Lords was reason enough for the dismissal of the Ministry. He did not think the supposed objection of the King to Lord John Russell, as leader of the House of Commons, was reason enough for breaking up the Administration. He did not think the time was fitting for the breaking up of an Administration; and if it had to be broken up, he would have preferred that the event had been brought about by any other cause than the personal intervention of the Sovereign. Moreover, he had very little hope indeed that the Ministry which he could form would be strong and stable— would even command such a majority in the House of Commons as would enable it to carry on the business of the country. These were not encouraging auspices under which to make the attempt; but Peel felt constrained by a sense of public duty—at all events, of duty to the Sovereign—to put all personal considerations aside, and go at the distasteful and unhopeful work.

Peel began by inviting Lord Stanley and Sir James Graham to join his Administration. Both declined the invitation. Sir James Graham promised, although he could not take office, to lend to Peel all the support he could, consistently with his own principles and opinions. Lord Stanley wrote to Peel a long and a very interesting letter. He pointed out that between Peel and himself there was, and always had been, a complete difference of opinion on almost every public question, except alone as regarded the Established Church. He reminded Peel that, so lately as on the occasion of Lord Grey's retirement from office, the Duke of Wellington seized the opportunity of passing in review the whole policy of the Whig Ministry, and condemned, not merely the Reform Act, but all the home and foreign policy of Lord Grey's Government. It was true, as Lord Stanley admitted, that Peel himself had passed no such sweeping censure on Lord Grey's measures. But he had opposed many of them in detail, and some of them in principle, and he had objected to the whole scope and tendency of the foreign policy. 'A few months only have elapsed; the Duke of Wellington is the person who, on the dissolution of Lord Melbourne's Cabinet, received the first mark of his Majesty's confidence; this circumstance alone must stamp upon the Administration about to be formed the impress of his name and principles.' 'You will not mistake me,' Lord Stanley went on, 'if I say that private feeling, as well as political judgment, alike disincline me to the adoption of this proposal.' Then follows a weighty sentence, which those who remember Lord Stanley can almost think they hear him delivering: 'The sudden conversion of long political opposition into the most intimate alliance, no general coincidence of principle, except upon one point, being proved to exist between us, would shock public opinion, would be ruinous to my own character, and injurious to the Government which you seek to form.' Nor can we refrain from quoting yet another sentence: 'If any beneficial moral effect were produced by my separation from Lord Grey and my former colleagues, and my abandonment of office for the sake of conscience and principle, that effect would he wholly destroyed by my speedy return to office with their political opponents.'

Sir Robert Peel then formed the best Ministry he could. He undertook the duties of First Lord of the Treasury and Chancellor of the Exchequer. Lord Lyndhurst was Lord Chancellor, and the Duke of Wellington became Foreign Secretary. Some new names come out in this Administration. Mr Gladstone was appointed Junior Lord of the Treasury; Winthrop Mackworth Praed, the young Tory poet of society, and Sidney Herbert, afterwards a leading statesman in the House of Commons, were made joint Secretaries of the Board of Control. It was held necessary, on various grounds of public convenience, that an appeal should be made to the country, and, accordingly, Parliament was dissolved. Peel issued an address to his constituents of Tamworth which was in itself an important political manifesto. At that time, and down to the end of his career, Peel made it a habit to convert his electioneering addresses into political manifestations. These documents rise altogether above the level of electioneering literature; they are historical publications. In this particular address Peel frankly announced that he considered the Reform Bill a 'final and irrevocable' settlement of a great constitutional question—'a settlement which no friend to the peace and order of the country would attempt to disturb, either by direct or by insidious means.' 'I never will admit,' he said, 'that I have been, either before or after the Reform Bill, the defender of abuses or the enemy of judicious reforms.' Of course, when Peel described the Reform Act as a final and irrevocable settlement of a great constitutional question, he did not mean to say that, in his opinion, Reform was never to march a step further. Peel was one of the last men to believe in the possibility of any one generation settling the business of all succeeding generations. He no more meant to convey the impression that Reform had spoken its last word, than Lord John Russell did when, addressing himself merely to the business of the passing day, he spoke of 'finality' in reforming legislation. What Peel meant was, that the decision of the Parliament and the people against the old, unreformed system was final and irrevocable. *Vestigia nulla retrorsum.* There was no going back, and no patriotic Englishman must endeavour, openly or secretly, to restore the system which the country had sentenced and doomed. Peel had already, in the House of Commons, expressed the same conviction. He spoke in the debate on the Address in the first session of the first Parliament assembled under the Reform Act. This was in January, 1833. He then declared that he considered the question of Reform as finally and irrevocably disposed of. He added, that he was for 'reforming every institution that really required reform, but he was for doing it gradually, dispassionately, and deliberately, in order that the reform might be lasting.' Even already, then, Peel had distinctly severed himself from the old-fashioned Toryism. The declaration of the Duke of Wellington with regard to Reform made in the September of 1830 was already a curious anachronism. The Duke of Wellington himself would not discourse in such a spirit to the House of Lords of 1834.

Parliament was dissolved in December 1834, and the new Parliament met in February 1835. The result was unsatisfactory to the Government. The Conservatives had gained, indeed, and gained very considerably in strength, but they were still in a minority. When the first Reformed Parliament met the Conservatives were in a perfectly miserable minority. The Liberals were estimated to have 486 votes, and the Conservatives only 172. Now there was indeed a change, for the Conservatives had 273, and the Liberals only 380. This was an advance to be sure; but, at the same time, it was rather a tantalising advance. A majority of 100 is just as good as a majority of 200. Once the majority gets above that level when a chance may pull it down, it does not matter, so far as opponents are concerned, what its precise numbers may be. Sir Robert Peel saw at once that he was doomed to a dreary and a hopeless task—dreary because hopeless. He was at the mercy of the Opposition. The Liberals could batter about his Administration in any way they pleased. It is hardly possible to imagine a situation more trying to a sensitive and high-spirited statesman, than to have to carry on a Government while his followers are in a minority, and with the bitter knowledge that, do what he will, his enemies have the power at any moment to undo his work.

The Opposition soon gave the Government a taste of their quality. Parliament met on February 19, and the first trial of strength was on the election of Speaker. The Government candidate was beaten by a majority of 10. This was a very small majority, all things considered and there was a peculiarity about its constitution which was significant, and which exhibited a political phenomenon very familiar indeed in more recent times. It was the Irish votes that decided the triumph of the Liberal candidate. The House of Commons then knew that the Liberals had secured the support of O'Connell and his party.

Bad began for Peel, and worse remained behind. The Government were defeated in the debate on the Address in the House of Commons, on an amendment censuring them for the dissolution. The majority against them was still very small—only 5; and again the victory, such as it was, showed itself to be the work of the Irish vote. Still, the defeat was annoying, and even damaging. Hardly less damaging was a victory which Peel won, by the help of Lord John Russell and some of the Liberals, over his own followers, on a motion for the repeal of the malt tax. Then, again, the strong opinions expressed in the House of Commons as to the appointment to the Embassy in St Petersburg of the Marquis of Londonderry, who had made himself highly unpopular, both by his denunciations of the English reformers and the Polish patriots, rendered it necessary that Lord Londonderry should resign the position. This, of course, was a vexatious blow to the Ministry. Peel bore up with courage and equanimity. He did not believe that his duty would allow him to resign office merely because of goads or pinpricks like these. He did not like to advise another dissolution, although another dissolution would in all probability tend to strengthen his hands. He kept bringing in Bills for what may be called moderate reform in various departments, especially in the ecclesiastical courts and Church discipline. He met the attacks, the questionings, and the obstruction of his antagonists with consummate skill and coolness. His skill as a leader was never more conspicuously shown than during his short and precarious term of office. Now, also, he had again an opponent worthy of his weapon. Now, once again, the strife of parties in the House of Commons had become typified—a great political and oratorical duel between the two leaders. Lord John Russell, called to the responsibility of commanding the forces of Opposition, had suddenly developed a wholly unexpected skill and power in debate. He showed himself well able to hold his own, even against the best efforts of Sir Robert Peel. Many years later, Lord John Russell himself wrote that he never had so hard a task to perform as the task of leading his party through all that keen series of encounters with the skill and experience of Peel. But the struggle had to come to an end. Peel fought his losing battle as gallantly and brilliantly as Napoleon conducted his retreat before the advancing armies of the Allies. But the end was certain in the one case as in the other. In April, 1835, Lord John Russell carried against the Government a motion to the effect that the surplus revenues of the Irish Church ought to be appropriated to general moral and religious purposes. The motion was carried by 285 votes against 258. This was the *coup de grâce*. Peel resigned, and passed into Opposition once again.

XII

The Irish Famine

Lord Melbourne Prime Minister—Death of William IV and accession of
Queen Victoria—The Jamaica Act—The ladies of the bedchamber—The
Whigs fall, and Peel comes in again—The Corn Law question comes up—The
Irish famine

L ORD MELBOURNE'S SECOND ADMINISTRATION WAS very like Lord
Melbourne's first, with, however, one remarkable exception—Lord
Brougham was not a member of it. From that time forth, during all his long
career, he never held office in any Government. There has been much speculation
as to the reason why the Whigs not only deprived themselves of the assistance of
Lord Brougham's great eloquence, influence, and energy, but turned these powers against themselves; and it was even at one time conjectured that there were
seasons in Brougham's life when his mental faculties were not altogether under
his control. But there does not seem any reason to hazard any such conjecture, or
to go beyond Lord Melbourne's spoken and written explanations. Before there
seemed any immediate prospect of the Whigs coming back to office, Melbourne
had made up his mind that he would have nothing more to do with Brougham.
In fact, Brougham was a man with whom nobody could get on. He had an
overbearing and even ferocious temper, and he had no idea of dignity, propriety,
or prudence. He used to stump the country after the fashion of O'Connell, and
deliver harangues such as, according to the etiquette of that time, an ex-Lord
Chancellor was not supposed to deliver. He was always getting into quarrels, and
always making compromising strokes off his own bat. Cast off by the Whigs, he
for a time forbore to attack them, but after this season of patience he joined with
Lord Lyndhurst in harassing, denouncing, and tormenting them.

Sir Robert Peel played a steady and a waiting game. He dealt fairly, and
even generously, with the Ministers; but he was biding his time. The King

hated his present advisers, and made no secret of his hatred. For a long time he would not even invite one of them to dinner. At length he relaxed, and gave them all an invitation, expressing on one occasion a hope, in his letter of invitation, that they would each man drink two bottles of wine. Peel and Lord John Russell felt a kind of dislike and distrust of each other. Both were shy and sensitive men, and for that reason were kept apart. That fact, however, did not prevent each from paying ready and generous tribute to the abilities of the other. Lord John Russell wrote once in positively enthusiastic admiration of a speech of Peel's which went near to shattering the Whig Administration. In truth, the Ministers were terribly over-weighted in both Houses so far as debating powers were concerned. In the House of Lords they had Brougham and Lyndhurst to encounter, and Lord Melbourne was but a poor speaker. In the House of Commons they had to bear the attacks of Peel, Graham, and afterwards Lord Stanley, and they had only one man of first-class debating power—Lord John Russell. Peel was gradually forming a strong Conservative party—not a Tory party. He was making himself strong in the country as well as in Parliament. He foresaw the time when he should be able to command a majority in the House of Commons.

Meantime an event occurred which had much effect on the conditions of government in Great Britain. On June 20, 1837, William IV died, and Queen Victoria came to the throne. The Duke of Wellington thought the accession of a woman to the sovereign's place would be fatal to the present hopes of the Tories. 'Peel,' he said, 'has no manners, and I have no small talk.' He seemed to take it for granted that the new Sovereign would choose her Ministers as a school-girl chooses her companions. He did not know, did not foresee, that with the accession of Queen Victoria the real reign of constitutional government in these islands was to begin. The late King had advanced somewhat on the ways of his predecessors, but his rule was still, to all intents and purposes, a personal rule. With the accession of Victoria the system of personal rule came to an end.

The elections which at that time were necessary on the coming of a new sovereign went slightly in favour of the Tories. The Whigs had many troubles. They were not reformers enough for the great body of their supporters. They made, or, perhaps, one should rather say, accepted, many great and noble reforms in political and social affairs; but all these had to be pressed upon them from without. The Radicals had split off from them. They could not manage O'Connell. The Chartist fire was already burning. There was many a serious crisis in foreign policy—in China and in Egypt, for example. The Canadian Rebellion and the mission of Lord Durham involved the Whigs in fresh anxieties, and laid them open to new attacks from their enemies. On the top of all came some disturbances, of a legislative rather than an insurrectionary kind, in Jamaica, and the Government felt called upon to bring in a Bill to suspend for five years the Constitution of the island. A Liberal and reforming Ministry bringing in a Bill to suspend a Constitution is in a highly awkward and dangerous position. Peel saw his opportunity, and opposed the Bill. The Government won by a majority of only 5. Lord Melbourne accepted the situation, and resigned. The Queen sent for the Duke of Wellington, and he, of course, advised her to send for Peel.

When Peel came, the young Queen told him with all the frankness of a girl that she was sorry to part with her late Ministers, and that she did not disapprove of their conduct, but that she felt bound to act in accordance with constitutional usages. Peel accepted the task of forming an Administration. And then came the famous dispute known as 'the Bedchamber Question'— the *question de jupons*. The Queen wished to retain her ladies-in-waiting; Peel insisted that there must be some change. Two of these ladies were closely related to Whig statesmen whose policy was diametrically opposed to that of Peel on no less important a question than the government of Ireland. Peel insisted that he could not undertake to govern under such conditions. The Queen, acting on the advice of her late Ministers, would not give way. The whole dispute created immense excitement at the time. There was a good deal of misunderstanding on both sides. It was quietly settled, soon after, by a compromise which the late Prince Consort suggested, and which admitted that Peel had been in the right. For the moment, however, it became a stormy controversy, and even Peel himself declaimed over it in language of almost extravagant rhetorical exaggeration. Its importance to us now is that, as Peel would not give way, the Whigs had to come back again, and they came back discredited and damaged, having, as Mr Molesworth puts it, got back 'behind the petticoats of the ladies-in-waiting.'

We may pass rapidly over the remaining history of the Whig Ministry. The Anti-Corn Law agitation had begun, and the Whigs made some tentative, ineffective efforts to go a little way in the direction of the new movement. Peel soon saw that their force was spent—that his time had come. He encountered them with a direct declaration of want of confidence, and defeated them by one vote. Ministers resigned, and appealed to the country, and the result of the general elections brought Peel back to office, and something more than office—it brought him back to power. He was at the head of a majority. Lord Melbourne resigned. Peel formed an Administration in which he had the co-operation of Lord Stanley and Sir James Graham.

The elections which brought Peel into power brought Richard Cobden for the first time into Parliament; and the great Free Trade struggle was about to begin.

The story of Sir Robert Peel's Administration in its dealing with the Corn Laws is a story of bitter and passionate controversy. Peel's enemies tell it in the shortest way. Peel, they say, came into power pledged to retain the Corn Laws, and in 1846 he repealed them. Let us examine the history of that eventful period a little more carefully. One part of the controversy at least has been entirely swept out of the way. No one now wants to offer or to listen to any argument for or against the principle of Free Trade. What we are concerned in is the personal conduct of Peel in the decisive part which he took.

What were the Corn Laws, to begin with? Old abuses are so soon forgotten that it is quite possible some of the younger generation may have only a very vague idea as to what the Corn Laws actually were. The Corn Law of 1815 was a copy of the Corn Law of 1670—so little had economic science grown in England during all those years. The Corn Law of 1670 imposed a duty on the importation of foreign grain which amounted almost literally to a prohibition. It was lawful to export wheat on payment of 1s. per quarter Customs duty; but the importation of wheat was virtually prohibited until the price of our own wheat at home had risen to 80s. a quarter. Such legislation was, of course, founded on the principle that the corn grew for the benefit of the grower in the first instance, and that, until a handsome profit had been secured to him, the public had no right to any reduction in the cost of food. When the harvest was good, then the grower began to get frightened, and he appealed to Parliament to protect him against the disaster of having to sell his corn any cheaper than in a year of scarcity or even of famine. It has been said, and said well, that 'the history of agricultural distress is the history of agricultural abundance.' This might seem at first a paradox, but it is not so; it is a truth that goes to the very heart of Protection. The Corn Law of 1815 was hurried through Parliament. It re-enacted the provisions of the former measure, and declared the practical prohibition of the entry of grain from foreign ports until the price of our own corn here at home had reached the magical figure of 80s. a quarter. But the commercial and manufacturing classes had had some education forced on them in the meantime. Great manufacturing towns like Manchester had always been for Free Trade. They wanted to sell their goods in every market where buyers were to be met, and they found themselves hampered at every turn by prohibitive legislation. The principle which captured so many other intelligences—the principle that by everybody paying a little too high a price for every article everybody will grow rich in turn—did not fall in with the practical experiences of Manchester.

In places like Manchester, when there was depression of trade, they could not see that the working-men were really any the better off for having to pay unnaturally high prices for their bread, while having at the same time to put up with reduced wages. Therefore, communities like Manchester were, from the very nature of their condition, driven early into scepticism as to the beauties and virtues of Protection.

The passing of the measure of 1815 was not accomplished without popular tumult. The poor man might not be much of a political economist, but he knew when his bread was too dear, and he knew that its price was put up by law for the benefit of the landlord class. There were riots here and there—very serious riots in some places. As in the Reform Bill riots, the houses of unpopular men were attacked. Incendiary fires blazed through the night. Then there were trials and executions. Men who had rushed into riot under the terrible impulse of hunger and despair were found guilty and hanged. Thus order was restored, and all went merrily again.

Attempts were made from time to time to modify the rigidity of the Corn Act by the adoption of sliding-scale measures, having for their object to set up a varying system of duty, so that the duty on foreign wheat should sink in proportion according as the price of home-grown wheat increased above a certain amount. There was really no difference in principle between the fixed duty and the sliding-scale; each alike sought to secure an enhanced price for the grower at the expense of the community. We need not find too much fault with the corn-growing class—that is, with the landlords; they followed the instincts of their class interests, just as all other orders of men are inclined to do. Later on, it was found that every class in turn resisted the application of the principle of free competition to its own saleable articles. But the misfortune in the case of the corn-growing interest was that the corn-growers were mainly the law-makers, and had it in their power to suit their own interests in imperial legislation. Gradually a Free Trade organisation began to be formed in and around Lancashire. This Free-trade organisation had its beginning in agricultural distress, and won its final triumph by means of agricultural distress. The Anti-Corn Law League was formed in Manchester. The great Free Trade Hall was built on the ground which we have already said was the scene of the massacre of Peterloo. A regular propaganda was set on foot for the education of the people in the gospel of Free Trade. The agitation caught fire. Among the first men of great popular influence who gave it a cordial co-operation was Daniel O'Connell. The Free Trade cause became a Parliamentary question. For several years the movement in the House of Commons was led by Mr Charles Villiers, a man of great ability and sound judgment. He was an aristocrat by family, but was strongly in sympathy with the English democracy. After a while he was, joined in the House of Commons by Mr Cobden and Mr Bright. Never had a great social and political cause two more fitting leaders than these two. All that argument and persuasion could do was the natural work of Cobden; all that oratory of the very first order could accomplish was accomplished by Bright.

A man like Peel could not see without the deepest interest, and without a growing sympathy, the rise of this great agitation. He knew the labouring class, he knew the artisan class. He had, under a chill and proud exterior, a singularly sensitive and benevolent heart. The whole turn of his intellectual training had set him against the fascinating sophistries of Protection. Sir Lawrence Peel says of him that he had always been a Free-trader. 'The questions to which he declined to apply those principles had been viewed by him as exceptional. The Corn Law had been so treated by many able exponents of the principle of Free Trade.' Sir Robert Peel had again and again expressed in the House of Commons his conviction, as to the general soundness of the principle of Free Trade. But he had up to this time always maintained that the Corn Laws and the Sugar Duties were exceptions to the common rule. It may once more be pointed out here, that it was not part of Peel's habit as a statesman to look far ahead. He waited until an event came up before he studied, and scrutinised it, and questioned it as to its significance and its meaning. To find fault with this tendency on the part of a great working statesman is to find fault with the very conditions of his work. He has no more time to speculate as to far distant phenomena than the steersman has to make calculations about the reappearance of some far distant eclipse.

There was nothing as yet to give Peel any serious warning that the time was close at hand when the question of Free Trade would have to be faced. Although the agitation was spreading so broadly in many of the great towns, it had as yet got little grasp of the House of Commons. It was hardly taken seriously there by the majority of members. The landlords themselves were not as yet in the least afraid of it. Mr Villiers, Mr Cobden, Mr Bright, Mr Milner Gibson, Mr W. J. Fox, and a few others, were its avowed champions. It is a fact of some significance, that the Anti-Corn Law League were not in the least discouraged by the advent of Peel to power. The leaders of that party did not profess any unqualified devotion to the Ministry of Lord Melbourne or Lord John Russell. They wanted the Minister, whoever he might be, who would give them Free Trade. They saw very soon that Peel was, on the whole, the most likely man. In the very debate which took place on the resignation of the Melbourne Ministry, Mr Cobden, who had just entered Parliament for the first time said 'I am a Free-trader—I call myself neither Whig nor Tory. I am proud to acknowledge the virtue of the Whig Ministry in coming out from the ranks of the monopolists, and advancing three parts out of four in my direction. Yet, if the right honourable baronet opposite (Sir Robert Peel) advances one step farther, I shall be the first to meet him half-way, and shake hands with him.' Some time later, Cobden, speaking at Birmingham, said: 'There can be no doubt that Sir Robert Peel is at heart as good a Free-trader as I am. He has told us so in the House of Commons again and again; nor do I doubt that Sir Robert Peel has in his inmost heart the desire to be the man who shall carry out the principles of Free Trade in this country.' When we read assertions that Peel had betrayed his party, it is surely of some importance to point to the fact that, so far back as 1841, the leader of the Free Trade agitation recognised Peel as a Free-trader. It is clear that even then Peel held opinions, and had often avowed them, which were absolutely irreconcilable with those of the ordinary Protectionist member of Parliament, and that he had done all he could to make these opinions of his known to the House of Commons. Outside the ranks of the Free Trade party, no one went really any further than Peel. Peel had up to this time contended that grain in England was a necessary exception to the general principle of Free Trade. Lord John Russell was not of opinion that the time had come when it could be treated as anything but an exception. If that be any real difference, such, and nothing else, was the difference between them. The Free-traders cared as little for Russell's fixed duty as for Peel's sliding-scale.

It would, perhaps, have been better in the end if Peel had been somewhat more of an effusive nature about this period of his career. If he had talked more freely with some of his colleagues—had unbosomed himself frankly and frequently, let them see the working of his mind, such open communion with them might have greatly helped to educate his party. But Peel was a shy and silent man. He thought questions over, and thought them out for himself, and seldom talked over them with any one until he himself saw his whole way clear before him. It is quite certain that he had not in 1841 even begun to see his way. In 1842 Peel introduced his proposals for a sliding-scale. Lord Melbourne in the House of Lords, and Lord John Russell in the House of Commons, proposed amendments in favour of a fixed duty, but they were defeated. Lord Melbourne, indeed, was very half-hearted about the matter. He told Lord John Russell that, while he did not think they ought to abandon the principle of a fixed duty, he did not suppose they could find anything particularly new or strong to say against the sliding-scale as Peel had arranged it. So lately as 1839 Lord Melbourne had declared, in the course of a debate in

the House of Lords, that 'to leave the whole agricultural interest without protection—I declare before God that I think it the wildest and maddest scheme
that it has ever entered into the imagination of man to conceive.' Of course,
the amendments were defeated, and Peel carried his sliding-scale. Mr Villiers
and Mr Cobden brought forward motions for repeal of the Corn Laws and
motions for inquiry into their working, but defeat only followed defeat.

On the 5th of January, 1843, Lord Melbourne wrote to Lord John Russell
asking him what language the Opposition intended to hold about corn when
the Parliament met. 'Of course,' Lord Melbourne writes, 'you have dismissed
from your mind the notion that the Government will move upon that subject. Peel would be an imbecile if he were to break up his party, and probably
his Administration, in that manner. He will remain quietly in his present
position. If I were he, I should not mind the Anti-Corn League and their
abettors.' Melbourne was not a very clear-seeing prophet. A month later
he writes to Lord John Russell, that 'Peel evidently means to side with the
strongest about corn. Robarts tells me the opinion in the City is that the
Corn Laws are doomed. Still, if the country is quiet, and the League lose
their popularity, he will stick by his law.' It is evident, then, that there was a
growing feeling that Peel was likely to go far towards the policy of repealing
the Corn Laws. The very earnestness with which Lord Melbourne expresses
his disbelief in such a purpose on Peel's part, only shows that the belief must
have been taking hold of the public mind. Melbourne was not a person to
understand the feelings of a man like Peel. He could not believe that anybody
who could command a majority in the House of Commons would think of
breaking up an Administration and a party for the sake of any reform whatever. Still, there is the plain fact that in 1843 Melbourne felt bound to combat,
with an earnestness very unusual in him, the growing idea that Peel was about
to join hands with the Free-traders, though by so doing he should break up
his party, and, as Lord Melbourne put it, even his Administration. It seems
hard to understand how any of Peel's own followers should never have found
any doubt or question arising in their minds upon the subject. It seems hard
to understand how they could have been so completely taken by surprise,
as they said they were, some years later, when Peel announced that he had
become a convert to the principles of Free Trade.

'Famine,' said Mr Bright many years afterwards, 'against which we had
warred, joined us.' In the autumn of 1845 the potato disease broke out in
Ireland, and the staple food of a whole population was gone almost in a
breath. Peel took from the first outbreak of the disease the deepest and most
anxious interest in the condition of Ireland. He had reports sent into him,

from all manner of sources, every day, on what he called 'the awful question of the potato crop in Ireland.' Never was a statesman filled with a profounder sense of responsibility. The Cabinet began to hold meeting after meeting in rapid succession. The Anti-Corn Law League were crying out for the opening of the ports. Peel himself was strongly in favour of the opening of the ports. He urged upon his colleagues the imperative necessity of removing all restrictions upon the importation of foreign grain, either by an Order in Council or by calling Parliament together, and recommending such a course in the Speech from the Throne. Peel was very frank with his colleagues. He expressed a strong doubt as to whether it would be possible, when once the ports had been opened, ever to close them again. Indeed, the Anti-Corn Law League were crying out for the opening of the ports on the express ground that, once opened, they never could be closed again. The doubt was enough for some of Peel's colleagues. The Duke of Wellington and Lord Stanley declared against the proposition, and Peel's wise policy fell through for the moment. 'The Cabinet,' says Peel himself, 'by a very considerable majority declined giving its assent to the proposals which I thus made to them. They were supported by only three members of the Cabinet—the Earl of Aberdeen, Sir James Graham, and Mr Sidney Herbert. The other members of the Cabinet, some on the ground of objection to the principle of the measures recommended, others upon the ground that there was not yet sufficient evidence of the necessity for them, withheld their sanction.' Peel knew that he was right, knew that events would soon show with a terrible earnestness how entirely right he was. But the Cabinet wanted educating as yet, and Peel could do nothing. He wrapped himself up in his usual proud patience, and he waited. Meantime the famine went stalking on.

XIII

Triumph and Fall

The Anti-Corn Law League—Peel announces his change of policy—He carries
Free Trade at last, but falls in his hour of triumph

THE COUNTRY WAS WAKING UP to a sense of the danger. Great organisations were being formed everywhere for the purpose of fighting the Irish famine by the arms of private beneficence and liberality. It is, perhaps, worth mentioning that one noble Duke wrote to Peel to say that, considering the rebellious spirit which the Irish people had long been showing, he did not think the Government ought to do anything to relieve their distress. Apparently, he was of opinion that the Government ought to leave them to stew in their own grease—to use the phrase of Chaucer which Prince Bismarck has brought to the knowledge of Englishmen. Let us do justice, however, to our noble Duke. He did not propose that Ireland should be actually left to starve—he was entirely in favour of private relief organisation but he thought the Government, as a Government, ought to take no steps to keep the contumelious people from starvation. One can imagine the feeling of compassion and contempt with which Peel must have studied such a communication.

Suddenly, Lord John Russell wrote a letter from Edinburgh to his constituents in the City of London—a letter which marks an epoch in the great Anti-Corn Law controversy. Lord John Russell announced that he had become a convert to the principles of the League. It was no longer worthwhile, he declared, to contend for a fixed duty. He denounced the Corn Law system in language as strong as Cobden, or even as Bright, could have used. He added a remark the significance of which is important to the readers of this volume—a remark to the effect that the Prime Minister seemed to be only waiting for some excuse to get rid of the whole system, and he called upon the people everywhere to give him that excuse by petition, by address, by remonstrance. Here, again, we have evidence to the fact, most important for a fair judgment as to Peel's whole course of action, that almost everybody outside the ranks of Peel's own party seems to have been satisfied that Peel desired nothing better than to have a chance of abolishing the Corn Laws.

We have not the smallest doubt that Peel welcomed Lord John Russell's letter with the most cordial satisfaction. It gave him just the excuse which he desired. Of all the arguments which a Prime Minister can use in order to prevail upon certain of his colleagues to assist him in introducing some measure which they disapprove of or distrust, there is none half so strong as the argument that, if we do not introduce it, the other men will. Of course, this argument would not have any influence over a man like Lord Stanley, for instance, who, although occasionally light-headed enough, yet would cling to a principle which he believed to be right, and would not allow the thought of holding on to office a feather's weight in his consideration. But the ordinary member of an Administration hates to be driven from office, and is almost invariably borne down by the appeal, 'What is the use in our holding back? If we do not do this thing, the men opposite will and they will come over here to do it, and take our places.' Peel must have felt that he had got a splendid weapon into his hand when Lord John Russell wrote that famous letter. Behold, here is the foremost man in the Opposition, and he declares in favour of repealing the Corn Laws, the Anti-Corn Law party will be ready enough to form a coalition with him, and against us. The thing will be carried anyhow, whether we like it or not. Why should not we form the coalition, and carry it?

There was, probably, no need for Peel to enforce these arguments in express words. They enforced themselves from the lines of Lord John Russell's letter. Peel has set forth very clearly in his *Memoirs*, and with all his accustomed candour, the influence which the letter of Lord John Russell had upon his own counsels and the counsels of his Cabinet. The letter did not hurry Peel on the way to Free Trade. As he says himself, a mere comparison of dates will show that his mind was made up before Lord John's letter had been written. He had endeavoured to persuade his colleagues to adopt a certain course, which course he told them plainly must conduct to Free Trade. He had made the effort, and failed, at the meeting of the Cabinet on Thursday, the 6th of November. Lord John Russell's letter was dated 'November 22.' But the effect which Lord John Russell's letter undoubtedly had was to satisfy Peel and the more thoughtful among Peel's colleagues that the coming of Free Trade was made certain, and that there was no reason why those who had always yearned for it, as Peel had always done, should balk their own chance, and feebly allow it to be carried by others.

Some of the humorous side of Peel's character comes out in his comments on the correspondence which he had to carry on at that time. Lord Kenyon, for example, suggested, among other measures which he believed calculated to relieve the distress in Ireland, 'a special public acknowledgment of our dependence on God's mercy in our present depressed state.' Peel makes on that suggestion the dry comment that a Minister might think it hardly consistent with reason to 'make a public acknowledgment of our dependence on God's mercy, and at the same time leave in full operation the restraints which man had imposed upon the import of provisions.'

A Cabinet Council was held on November 25, almost immediately after the publication of Lord John Russell's letter. Peel recommended the summoning of Parliament at once, for the purpose of taking measures to relieve the distress in Ireland, but also for the purpose of announcing some legislation designed, either to repeal the Corn Laws, or to prepare the way for their repeal. He was now quite satisfied that the Protection system had utterly broken down, and that the sooner it was got rid of, the better. Lord Stanley could not yet see his way. He asked for time to consider, and, the more he considered, the more Protectionist he became. The Duke of Wellington took an attitude worthy of Colonel Newcome. He was quite unchanged, he declared, in his personal conviction that the Corn Laws ought to be maintained, but he frankly owned that he 'thought a good Government for the Queen was more important than Corn Laws or any other consideration.' He had convinced himself that Peel was the only man who could properly administer Government for the Queen, and, therefore, he was quite prepared to support every measure Peel thought it right to bring in. The Happy Warrior gave out his ideas with a touching simplicity. Perhaps there never was a more ingenuous avowal of the faith that man was made for the Government, and not the Government for man. Lord Stanley at last made up his mind that he could not remain in the Cabinet to carry out a policy which, to put it mildly, must at least end in the repeal of the Corn Laws. The Duke of Buccleuch was of the same conviction. In Peel's judgment, there was nothing for it now but to resign office. He did not feel that, deprived of such considerable support, he was in a position to carry out his policy. He might have resigned when, on the 5th of November, his colleagues declined to accept his recommendations. But he argued, very wisely and justly, then, that he was still bound to keep to his post. Not all of those who could not agree to his proposals had rejected them peremptorily and finally. It seemed quite probable that the teaching of events might school some of those who doubted into a better knowledge of the right course to be taken—might teach them, at all events, that the course recommended was

inevitable. But Peel made up his mind in the most decisive way that his reten-
tion of office for the time was merely to give others an opportunity of coming
round to him, and not with any idea whatever of his coming round to them.
'In determining,' he says, 'to retain office for the present, I determined also
not to recede from the position I had taken, and ultimately to resign office
if I should find, on the re-assembling of the Cabinet, that the opinions I
had expressed did not meet with general concurrence.' Now this condition
had been realised, and Peel would not hesitate. On December 5 he went to
Osborne, 'and humbly solicited her Majesty to relieve me from duties which I
felt I could no longer discharge with advantage to her Majesty's service.'

Peel acted rightly when he forbore to resign on the first rejection of his
advice by his colleagues, and rightly also when he determined to resign on
finding that he could not obtain the general concurrence of the Cabinet
after he had given his colleagues a second chance. He had one strong and
steady purpose in his mind, and that was to bring about the repeal of the
Corn Laws. That purpose dominated all his thoughts and all his actions.
He would stay in office, despite of every rebuff and every disappointment,
so long as he thought he could by staying in office help to repeal the Corn
Laws. He would not stay in office one moment after he had satisfied himself
that, for whatever reason, it was not in his power to repeal the Corn Laws.
After the Cabinet Council of November 25 he became convinced that the
work of repealing the Corn Laws was a man's office, but not his, as Beatrice
puts it; that Lord John Russell, with the Whigs, could do it. When he had
come to this conclusion, he at once resigned his place.

The Queen sent for Lord John Russell. Russell came up from Edinburgh,
and did his best to form an Administration. It was a difficult undertaking.
His party was in a minority in the House of Commons, and was not very
strong in the country. For some reason or other the elections which had
recently taken place here and there had not gone favourably for the Free-traders. Before making any attempt, Russell endeavoured to obtain from Peel a
promise that he would support a measure for the complete and immediate
repeal of the Corn Laws. Peel could not see his way to give any promise of
the kind, nor would he even consent to be consulted as to the draft scheme of
the measure. He did not think it would be proper on his part to give such a
pledge; and he did not think it would do any good to the common purpose,
but only harm, if he were to co-operate in the preparation of a scheme. He
was convinced that 'previous concert, or a previous pledge on his part to support any particular measure of adjustment, would be distasteful to the House
of Commons and embarrassing to all parties.' Lord John Russell admitted

the fairness of Peel's course of action, and, although terribly embarrassed by the task forced upon him, he still went to work, with undaunted and highly characteristic courage, to form an Administration. A new difficulty arose in his way. Lord Grey—lately Lord Howick, and who had just succeeded his father, the Lord Grey of the Reform Bill—refused to take office if Lord Palmerston, of whose policy he strongly disapproved, were to be Foreign Secretary. Lord Grey also held that Mr Cobden ought to be invited to take a seat in the Cabinet. Lord John Russell felt satisfied that the complete and cordial concurrence of all the leading men of his party would be necessary in order to give him the slightest chance of maintaining an Administration. This he found himself unable to secure, and, therefore, he said in his letter to the Queen, 'he must now consider that task as hopeless which has been from the beginning hazardous.' Peel had been sent for by the Queen for a parting interview on his retirement from office. To his surprise, he found on his arrival at Windsor that the Queen had now to invite him to resume office. He had no choice but to agree under such conditions, and he returned from Windsor on the evening of December 20 'having resumed all the functions of First Minister of the Crown.' He expressed his own feelings simply and frankly in a letter to the Princess Lieven. 'I resume power,' he wrote, 'with greater means of rendering public service than I should have had if I had not relinquished it. But it is a strange dream. I feel like a man restored to life after his funeral service had been preached.' The Duke of Buccleuch withdrew his opposition to Peel's policy, and consented to remain in office. Lord Stanley held to his resolve, and would have nothing to do with the Ministry. His place as Secretary for the Colonies was given by Peel to Mr Gladstone, who was now, like Peel himself, a convinced Free-trader. It is a curious fact that Mr Gladstone did not sit in Parliament during the eventful session that was coming. He had obtained a seat for the borough of Newark through the influence of the Duke of Newcastle; but the Duke of Newcastle had withdrawn his support from Peel, and Mr Gladstone therefore did not seek immediate re-election on accepting office, but remained for some months without a seat in the House of Commons. During his absence the great battle, in which he would have made a splendid figure, was fought and won.

Parliament met on the 22nd of January, 1846. The Speech from the Throne referred with satisfaction to the measures already taken from time to time to extend commerce and stimulate domestic skill and industry by the repeal of prohibitive and the relaxation of protective duties, and recommended Parliament to take into its early consideration whether 'the principle on which you have acted may not with advantage be yet more extensively applied.' Before the Address in reply to the Speech from the Throne was moved, Peel rose, and gave notice that he would on the earliest possible day submit to the consideration of the House certain measures connected with the commercial and financial affairs of the country. There was surprise, there was anxiety, when this brief announcement was made. Was that all the House was going to hear that night? Were the men to be sent home with absolutely unsatisfied anxiety? The Address was moved and seconded, and men tried to listen with fair appearance of interest; but everyone was think-ing about Peel and the Government, and what they were going to do. At last the formal speech-making was over, and the Speaker put the question from the chair. Then was the time for debate to begin—and there is always some debate, or, at least, some talk on the motion for the Address. Usually the leader of the Opposition begins—criticises the Ministerial policy, and gives the Ministers something to reply to. No one at that moment was look-ing with any expectation towards the Treasury Bench; most members were looking towards Lord John Russell or Mr Cobden. Suddenly, to the surprise of all, Sir Robert Peel himself got up, and then everyone knew that the great explanation was about to be made.

Even then, however, the full explanation did not come. Peel's speech was long, elaborate, tantalising. It was less of a Ministerial explanation or a Ministerial announcement of a coming policy than an *apologia pro vitâ suâ*—an account of the speaker's own conversion. It went into elaborate calculations, and arrayed masses of figures to show that reduction of duty was constantly followed by expansion of the revenue, and often even by a maintenance of high prices. One great fact, however, was made clear to both sides of the House: Sir Robert Peel had become a convert to the doc-trines of Cobden, and was for Free Trade *sans phrase*. The time had arrived when, in Peel's opinion, that protection on home-grown corn which he had come into power to maintain must be abandoned for ever. It was the story of Catholic Emancipation over again.

The debate of that opening night was made memorable by the first really successful speech which Disraeli ever delivered in the House of Commons. The speech was made just at the right moment: it found the Conservative party reeling and staggering it rallied them into a party once again. For an interval yet the Protectionists were to be led by Lord George Bentinck, but from the moment when Disraeli delivered his speech he was marked out as the real inspiration and guide of the party.

On the 27th of January Peel explained his financial policy. A sort of *ad interim* tariff, gradually declining, was to be kept up for three years, and at the end of that time protection on corn was to be abandoned altogether. That is the sum and substance of the announcement. It did not quite satisfy the Free-traders. They would, if they could, have had the abolition immediate. But although they proposed an amendment embodying their own views, they had, of course, no idea of not accepting cordially the reform which Peel was offering. The real struggle was on the amendment proposed by the Protectionists, which was simply a motion for the absolute rejection of the Government measure. The debate lasted twelve nights, and at the end the Protectionists were defeated by 337 votes against 240; a majority of 97. Large as this majority was, it was not quite so large as had been expected on both sides, and the result put the Protectionists into better spirits, and gave them courage to persevere in their resistance. The resistance now took the form of obstruction. There was ample room for obstruction, seeing that each of the two great financial proposals of the Government had to be introduced and carried as a separate Bill.

One painful scene during the course of the debates was caused by Disraeli—or rather, perhaps, we should say that a very painful incident in a former debate was revived by Disraeli. A few years before Peel's private secretary, Mr Edward Drummond, was shot dead by an assassin, who afterwards was proved to be a lunatic, and sent to an asylum for life. There could be no doubt that the attempt was intended for Peel himself. As was but natural, the event made a profound impression on Peel, and during one of the debates on Free Trade, before Peel had yet altered his policy, Cobden happened to say that he would hold the Prime Minister responsible for the condition of the country. Peel suddenly lost his temper and his self-control, and, jumping to his feet, declared that he understood Cobden to be threatening him with assassination. So high did men's passions run at the time, that the Tory benches rang with cheers for Peel as he made this frantic charge against a man of the noble and blameless character of Cobden. Of course, Peel, with his generous heart, soon repented of his inconsiderate outburst and his absurd charge; and the incident once passed, ought to have been allowed to lie buried in forgetfulness. Disraeli was ungenerous enough to make allusion to it in one of his attacks on Peel during the long debates on Peel's Free Trade measures. Perhaps, on the whole, it was well that the allusion should have been made. It only drew from Peel a renewed apology, and a renewed expression of regret for the charge he had made; and from Cobden a declaration that the apology was entirely satisfactory, and the expression of an earnest hope that no one on either side of the House would ever allude to the subject again. We have seen that Peel lost his temper during one of the debates on the Reform Bill;

and the truth is that, like many men who seem all chilliness and self-control, he had a sensitive nature and a quick temper, which only the pressure of an almost constant self-repression enabled him to keep under control. We need not go into the details of the long Parliamentary struggle. The Government measure passed its third reading, on May 5, by a majority of 98 votes. It then went up to the House of Lords, and by the earnest endeavours of the Duke of Wellington was carried through that House. It was read for the third time on June 25. But the final triumph of Peel's great policy was not the only event of June 25. That eventful day saw the success of Peel's policy and the fall of Peel's Administration. The battle was won; but the victor was in the dust.

Ireland caused the fall. During the course of the debates on the Corn Bill in the House of Commons, the Government believed it necessary to introduce a Coercion Bill for Ireland. This was a sort of policy which every Government then was in the habit of adopting. There was nothing remarkable in Peel's having recourse to it. But, of course, the Irish members—those who followed the leadership of O'Connell—would naturally oppose such a Bill. That was to be expected. Lord George Bentinck, the leader of the Protectionist party, supported the Coercion Bill in the first instance. During the Whitsuntide recess he changed his views. He declared that he had supported the Bill on the assurance of the Government that it was absolutely necessary for the safety of life in Ireland, but that the Government had shown that it was not a question of any urgency by the fact that they had not pressed the Bill forward in advance of all other legislation. Further, he added that he had no longer any confidence in the Government, and that he would not trust it with any extraordinary powers. Of course, the meaning of all this was obvious. The disappointed and angry Protectionists saw that there was a very good chance of defeating Peel on the Coercion Bill, and so turning him out of office. Mr Disraeli, in his *Life of Lord George Bentinck*, admits that 'the spirit of vengeance' had taken possession of the breasts of most of the party. The chance of obtaining retribution seemed to grow better and better as time went on. The Whigs, when in Opposition, generally refused to give their support to a mere scheme of coercion, unaccompanied by any remedial measures, and the new Radical party, who worked with Cobden and Bright, were almost certain to take that course now. No sense of gratitude to Peel for his Free Trade policy would prevent severely conscientious men like Cobden and Bright from voting against a measure of which they disapproved. In short, the Protectionists saw their chance, and were determined to avail themselves of it. Peel knew what was coming. He foresaw that he must be defeated, and he made up his mind that, if defeated, he would go out of office, and would not appeal to the country.

The Duke of Wellington was rather in favour of an appeal to the country, but Peel had made up his mind in advance. There was a clear interchange of views between Wellington and Peel on this subject, which may be read even now with deep interest—which, at least so far as Peel's part of the correspondence is concerned, is not without application to the politics of to-day. On the 21st of June Peel sent to the Duke a memorandum of his views as to the coming crisis. He indulged in no illusions; he was a man whose characteristic it was always to front the facts, and never to indulge in illusions. 'Depend upon it,' he wrote, 'that we shall not pass the Irish Bill into a law. If we have a small majority on the first division, it will give us no assurance, and, in my opinion, no hope of success. We shall be defeated by concerted delay, if we cannot be defeated by numbers.' There would be obstruction. Perhaps it might be thought that public opinion in England would put down the obstruction. 'Do not trust to this. There is an Irish party—a determined and not insignificant one—for which British indignation has no terrors.' What, then, was to be done? Ministers might make up their minds to dissolve Parliament, and appeal to the country instead of resigning. 'There is nothing I should deprecate more than dissolution of Parliament on the express ground of the Coercion Bill—of all the grounds, I think it the worst and the most dangerous.' First, he shows that it would only bring about a return of Irish members even more determined to oppose and obstruct Coercion Bills. 'But, secondly, let us beware for higher reasons how we make a dissolution of Parliament turn on a question between Great Britain and Ireland.' 'Shall Ireland be subject to a severe and unconstitutional law which is not to be applied, and never was applied, to Great Britain? It will be vain to say that our object is to protect life in Ireland. The answer will be that there are scarcely 20 out of 105 Irish members who agree with us in the necessity or probable efficacy of the measure. The Irish representative body is against us—is against an unconstitutional law intended separately for Ireland. The cry in England—if such a cry could be got up, or if it were decent or safe to attempt it—must be Coercion for Ireland. The cry in Ireland will be Equal Law—No Coercion. No Popery was a dangerous watchword for a general election. I firmly believe that the more dangerous watchword, Coercion for Ireland, would shake the foundations of the Legislative Union.' The point to which attention should be directed in this memorandum is the singular clearness with which Peel separates his own personal convictions from the manner in which public opinion will work, and from the results of that working. Peel never was much in sympathy with the national sentiment of Ireland. He was not able even to make much allowance for the position of the Irish members. He had very harsh words for them often. He had studied Ireland only from the windows of Dublin Castle. His particular friend, Mr Gregory, was much disliked by the Irish Catholics, and had no feeling for their cause or their claims. Peel was fully convinced that a Coercion Bill was needed for the preservation of life in Ireland. Yet he was able to detach himself absolutely from his own predilections and his own convictions, and to see distinctly what other people would think of the policy which he felt bound to advocate. Those Irish members whom I dislike and distrust—yet, are they not, after all, the representatives of the Irish people? Will not Englishmen ask how you come to bring in exceptional legislation for Ireland without consulting the Irish representatives, and obtaining their assent? This Coercion Bill is necessary; but it is a Bill which no one would think of applying to England, and it is, of course, unconstitutional—a suspension of the Constitution in Ireland. These Irish members, noisy, violent, obstructive—they do not care about the wrath of English public opinion, because they look only to the public opinion of their own country. If we do dissolve, the only cry we could raise would be the cry of Coercion for Ireland; to which Ireland would answer with the counter-cry of No Coercion—Equal Laws for the Two Countries. And which cry would tell with the more thrilling effect? The most ardent Irish Nationalist could hardly read that Memorandum of Peel's without a feeling of admiration for the logical courage and truthfulness of the man. He would not like Peel's way of speaking of the Irish representation; he would think Peel's style pathetic, prejudiced, and harsh as regarded Ireland; but he would admit that there were no shams about the great Minister. If Peel felt bound to thrust on Ireland exceptional legislation, he was at least incapable of making any pretence at believing it not exceptional. If the Constitution were to be suspended in Ireland, and not in England, he was utterly above the absurdity of pretending that equal legislation existed in the two countries. Nor did he for a moment think of disguising from himself the fact that, no matter how needful he might believe coercive laws for Ireland to be, the majority of the English people in their hearts distrusted and detested such legislation, and that it would not be good to face a general election with no better war-cry for the polls.

There was a long and an impassioned debate on the Coercion Bill. Peel's prophecy came to be realised to the full. The irreconcilables among the Protectionists voted with the Whigs and the Radicals and the Irish Nationalist members, and the Bill was defeated on its second reading by 292 votes against 219. The Ministry were left in a minority of 73. This was on

June 25, four days after the date of Peel's Memorandum. Eighty Protectionists followed Lord George Bentinck into the lobby, and their votes decided the fate of Ministers. Theirs was strictly and altogether a stroke of vengeance. Cobden preluded his vote by a warm eulogy of the manner in which Peel had fought and won his Free Trade battle. Lord George Bentinck declared, on behalf of his Protectionists, that 'it is time atonement should be made to the insulted country, to an insulted Parliament, and to the betrayed constituency of the Empire.' On the following Monday it was announced by the Duke of Wellington in the House of Lords, and Sir Robert Peel in the House of Commons, that the Ministers had tendered, and that the Queen had accepted, their resignation.

Disraeli has found fault with Peel's closing speech—the speech in which he announced his resignation of office. Public opinion has certainly not ratified Disraeli's assertion that it was a speech full of glorification and pique. It was, indeed, full of an emotion not common with Peel, but highly honourable and becoming; and it was modest and dignified. Nothing could be more generous than the tribute to Cobden, and the frank declaration that Cobden's name, and not Peel's own, would for ever be associated with the triumph of Free Trade. The closing passage of the speech may almost be considered already classic:—'It may be that I shall leave a name sometimes remembered with expressions of goodwill in those places which are the abode of men whose lot is to labour and to earn their daily bread by the sweat of their brow—a name remembered with expressions of goodwill when they shall recreate their exhausted strength with abundant and untaxed food, the sweeter because it is no longer leavened with a sense of injustice.'

XIV

The Last Chapter

*Peel's vindication of his policy—His position in the country—His seeming
prospects, and his sudden death*

S O THE GREAT CAREER WAS over—the great Minister had fallen. At the
moment of his most splendid triumph his enemies closed round him
and struck him down. 'We have fallen in the face of day,' Peel wrote to Lord
Hardinge in India, 'and with our front to our enemies.' The defeat took place
two hours after Peel had received the news that the Corn and the Customs
Bills had passed through the House of Lords. By another curious coincidence,
on the very day when he had to announce to the House of Commons the
resignation of the Government, the news arrived that the Oregon Question,
which at one time looked so serious, had been peaceably settled; that the
proposals of the Peel Government had been accepted in full by the United
States. The ambition of no English statesman could ask for a higher satisfaction than was contained in these two triumphs. No wonder that Peel should
have closed his letter to Lord Hardinge with the words:— 'Lady Peel and I are
here, quite alone, in the loveliest weather, feasting on solitude and repose, and
I have every disposition to forgive my enemies for having conferred upon me
the blessing of the loss of power.' A still more characteristic letter of Peel's is
published in his *Memoirs*. It is written in reply to the remonstrance of a noble
lord whose name is not given, and who found fault, not with the repeal of the
Corn Laws, but with the manner of bringing about the repeal. The author
of the remonstrance was of opinion that the result might have been brought
about without offending the Conservative party. He thought there should
have been confidential communications with certain peers and other leading Conservatives, and meetings to give and receive explanations—in other
words, that Peel ought to have educated the party. The question has often

been raised—will be raised again and again—Why did not Peel take his party into his confidence? Peel himself gives his reasons with great frankness, and they are, unquestionably, reasons of a highly practical character. In December, 1845, Peel tells us he had made up his mind that the repeal of the Corn Laws was 'indispensable to the public welfare, and to the real interest and security of the Protectionists themselves. Being of that opinion, every consideration became subordinate to the carrying of repeal. I was determined to carry it, for failure after proposing it would have involved this country in most serious evils.' Then comes a declaration which must at the time have been read with surprise:—'It was impossible to reconcile the repeal of the Corn Laws by me with the keeping together of the Conservative party, and I had no hesitation in sacrificing the subordinate object, and with it my own political interests.' Peel, then, knew clearly what he was doing. He knew that he was about to break up his party, knew that he was going to ruin his own political interests. A man must be a thorough partisan indeed who will not say that the Minister who has to choose between his party and his country is bound to one decision, and one only. Peel goes on to show the difficulties which stand in the way of conveying information to a political party as to the intentions of a Minister 'in regard to questions which are intimately connected with great commercial speculations and great pecuniary gains and losses'; and he declares that it is 'ten times more difficult to make such a communication to a selected few.' 'Times are changed since a Prime Minister, after ascertaining the sentiments of the Marquess of Hertford, and the Duke of Rutland, and the Earl of Lonsdale, could form a pretty good guess of the inclinations and probable conduct of a whole party.' 'There is not time for a Minister to hold separate communications with Lord This and Mr That, and go through the whole series of facts and arguments, the combination, the general result of which has led him to form a settled but still debateable conclusion. Nothing but the full and ample detail which can be made once for all in Parliament will do justice to the case, and gain the assent of reluctant supporters. I am perfectly satisfied that if, at any time between the 1st of November and the day on which (having resumed the Government, on which neither Lord John Russell nor Lord Stanley would venture) I announced in the House of Commons the intended repeal of the Corn Laws, I had tried to gain acquiescence, either by belabouring individuals separately, or by summoning the party generally, I should have received scarcely one promise of support. I should have had on the part of the most moderate a formal protest against the course I intended to pursue; to the most violent I should have given facilities for organised opposition; I should have appeared to be flying in the face of a whole party, and contumaciously disregarding their opinion and advice after I had professed to consult them; but (what is of infinitely more importance) I should have failed in carrying the repeal of the Corn Laws.'

This is Peel's final reply to the arguments of the noble man who remonstrated with him. 'I was resolved,' Peel says, 'not to fail. I did not fail; and if I had to fight the battle over again, I would fight it in the same way. Lord ——'s way was certain of defeat.'

It seems to me impossible to get over Peel's arguments, if once we accept the principle with which he starts, that he was bound to carry the repeal of the Corn Laws in that session of Parliament. But, as Peel very truly says, it would have been ruinous to the country to keep such a great financial revolution hanging over the heads of the people for session after session, while reluctant Tories were yielding slowly to conversion. What alternative course was left to him to adopt? It was clear that, as the conditions were, he was the only man who could play the game and win the victory. Lord John Russell did not see his way to make the attempt; and no one could question Russell's courage or patriotism. Lord Stanley did not see his way to form a Ministry which should satisfy the Protectionists; and certainly no one ever doubted Lord Stanley's courage or his zeal for Protection. What, then, did the Protectionist Tories complain of? That they were not consulted; that the measure was sprung upon them. Nothing is more difficult than to lay down any precise rule with regard to the duty of a Minister of State as regards consultation with the members of his party generally. It is every day growing more and more necessary that such consultations should be held as often as possible, and that the whole party should be taken as much as possible into the confidence of the leaders. So much is this necessity growing, that it will probably make itself a serious embarrassment to the leaders of parties in the future. The electors are ever so much more numerous than they were; the constituencies are better educated in politics, and more self-reliant: they watch with close scrutiny every movement of their representatives; they are no longer content to let a representative do the best he can for their interests, and ask no questions, trusting absolutely to his guidance; they would no longer be content with his assurance that he had followed his leader without knowing whither his leader proposed to go. Therefore, if the constituencies expect more from their representative, the representative, for his part, must ask more from his leader. It is easy to foresee that this must render the position of a leader more difficult in certain emergencies as time goes on. For there must always be seasons of crisis, when it becomes absolutely necessary for a statesman in office to prepare for a policy which it is absolutely necessary to keep from premature publicity. Take, for instance, some momentous question in foreign affairs. England is engaged in controversy with some great foreign power. The controversy thus far has been diplomatic and highly courteous on both sides, and everything appears to be going smoothly. But the English statesman has made up his mind that England's interests require that certain claims shall be yielded to her. He must face the consideration of what is to be done if these claims are not yielded. Shall he have to make war? Would anybody say that he ought to call a meeting of his party, and put the question to them for their decision? Would anybody argue that he ought to accept their decision? Would it be humanly possible to keep such a consultation and its purpose secret? And might not the news of such a consultation getting abroad be the very means of enabling the enemy to strengthen his position in time, and bid defiance to England's claims?

I feel the greatest sympathy with the desire of a political party to be taken into the confidence of their leaders. It is trying to be committed to some line of action on which one has never been consulted. But I do not see how a condition of things ever can arise which will enable a Minister to communicate with his party at every emergency. There must be times when a battle has to be fought without a council-of-war. The question to be considered in this instance is, whether the repeal of the protective tariff was an emergency of that kind. I think it clearly was. Peel could not have converted his party in time, if, indeed, he could ever have converted them, as a party, at all. The effort to get up a counter-revolution, a restoration of Protection, lasted for years after the passing of the measures introduced by Peel. Disraeli was the fiercest in denouncing Peel, on the ground that he had betrayed his party. Disraeli, long after, boasted that he himself had educated his party on the subject of Parliamentary reform. But he certainly did not consult his party as to the policy by which he allowed a very valueless scheme of so-called reform to be converted into a measure of household suffrage for cities and boroughs. The resolutions which he proposed to bring in at the opening of the session of 1867, and which he afterwards withdrew, laid down the very principles of the policy to which he invited the solemn sanction of the House of Commons. But the policy he ultimately carried out was based on entirely different, and positively antagonistic, principles. He did not consult his party on each change of front. He was himself being driven along—being educated, if that phrase seems better—and he had no time to stop on the way for the purpose of educating any one else. His people had to follow him, and that was all.

Therefore, I feel convinced that all impartial persons will give Peel the credit of having decided rightly at a great crisis. There was much bitterness of feeling at the time, even among men who did not belong to Peel's party, and could not complain that they had been betrayed. Lord Melbourne, in his usual rough way, declared that Peel had done 'a damned dishonest thing.' That sort of feeling soon wore away, and all men owned that Peel had acted in 'a general honest thought and common good to all.' And he had acted wisely—and he had carried Free Trade. It is characteristic of him that in the very closing agony of the Coercion Bill crisis he found time to listen to the appeals, and send money to the help of the unfortunate painter, Haydon.

Peel never was in office again. He bore his part in the great debate on Don Pacifico and his trumpery claims in June, 1850. The debate was made memorable by Lord Palmerston's speech, by the sudden leap into fame of the late Sir Alexander Cockburn, and by the melancholy fact that, during that debate, the House of Commons listened for the last time to the voice of Sir Robert Peel. Peel spoke firmly, strongly, eloquently in condemnation of the policy of Lord Palmerston. But he paid a warm and characteristic tribute to the marvellous skill and power displayed in Palmerston's speech—a speech which first told the House of Commons that it had in Palmerston a Parliamentary debater of the highest order. 'We are all proud of him,' Peel exclaimed. The debate closed on the morning of Saturday, June 29. It was nearly four o'clock when the House divided, and it was found that the policy of Palmerston in Greece had been sanctioned—or, perhaps, it would be more proper to say condoned—by a majority of 46. The sun was streaming into the corridors when Peel left the House of Commons—for ever. He went home, but had not much time for sleep. There was an important meeting of the Commissioners of the Great Industrial Exhibition—the first Exhibition, the famous Crystal Palace Exhibition—for twelve o'clock that day. The site of the building had to be decided on, and Prince Albert and the Royal Commissioners generally relied much on the influence of Peel to sustain them against a certain clamorous objection raised to the proposed site in Hyde Park. Peel was present at the meeting, and undertook to assume the leadership in defending the action of the Commissioners, if defence should be necessary, before the House of Commons. He returned home for a short time, and then went out for a ride in the Park. On Constitution Hill he stopped to exchange a word or two with a friend, a young lady, who was also on horseback. Peel's horse suddenly shied, and threw him off, and Peel clinging to the bridle the horse slipped, and came down on him. Such an accident happens almost every day without fatal result. It was not so destined for Peel. The horse came with its knees on Peel's shoulders, and the work was done. It was found at once that the injuries Peel had received were past all surgery. For two or three days he still lived—or, rather, still lingered in life; hovered about its dark and shadowy places. He was sometimes conscious, sometimes wholly delirious from mere pain. Nearly all the members of his family and some of his closest friends and political comrades were round his dying bed. About eleven o'clock on the night of July 2 the release came, and Peel was dead.

> Now is the stately column broke;
> The beacon-light is quenched in smoke,

to quote the lines from Sir Walter Scott which Mr Gladstone cited in the House of Commons when he spoke what may be called the funeral oration of his friend and leader. The Duke of Wellington paid a tribute in the House of Lords to the memory of the man he loved and revered—a tribute which, like that paid by Pericles on one famous occasion, was more eloquent than oratory of any order could be, for it broke down utterly in tears.

The nation mourned for Peel. Parliament and the country were ready to pay any homage to his memory. Lord John Russell, with the sanction of the Crown, offered that the remains of the great statesman should be buried with public honours in Westminster Abbey. But Peel had set out in his will his express desire that his body should lie with the coffins of his father and mother in the family vault at Drayton Bassett. All that the country could do was to give him a monument in the Abbey. A peerage was offered to Lady Peel, but, as might have been expected, was declined.

But for that stumbling horse Peel might yet have had a great career before him. The best of his life might have been to come. He was younger by some years when he died than Palmerston when he won his first great triumph in debate—that triumph to the splendour of which Peel had only just borne a generous tribute. It seems likely for many reasons that, if Peel had lived a little longer, he would have been called once again to preside over the councils of his Sovereign. Or it is possible that he might have taken the the position of unofficial adviser to the Sovereign. In either case he would have rendered high service to his country. His intellectual power was at its best when he was suddenly taken from life.

Peel was, undoubtedly, as Lord Beaconsfield has said, a great member of Parliament; but he was surely very much more than that; he was a great statesman, a great Minister. He must always rank among the foremost of English Ministers. The proud boast of Heine is that, if any one names the best half-dozen of German poets, his name must be brought in among them. If we name the best half-dozen of modern English Prime Ministers, we can hardly fail to bring in the name of Peel. The happy fortunes of his country deprived him of any chance of proving himself a really great man. Never since the time of the younger Pitt has England been tried by any danger which threatened for one moment her national position. Danger such as that proves a man, and, should he prevail over it, stamps him as one of Time's great men. Such a chance was given in our own days to Count Cavour, and to Prince Bismarck; and each man proved what he was worth. England is now too great, and strong, and happy, to give her statesmen any such chance. We can only be left to conjecture what they might have done if put to it. Peel's claim to the highest form and order of statesmanship is like Hamlet's claim to the soldier's music and the rights of war'—the claim that

> He was likely, had he been put on,
> To have proved most royally.

To every difficulty by which he was tried Peel proved himself equal; it was his own proud and honest boast that he had never proposed anything which he did not carry. Only the royal opportunity was needed for him to have proved himself most royally. It is to his eternal honour that he himself, by the wisdom and the high aim of his policy, helped to consolidate that national prosperity and that popular content whereby some of those dangers were averted which are the ordeal and the touchstone of the supreme order of statesmanship.

ALSO AVAILABLE FROM NONSUCH PUBLISHING

For forthcoming titles and sales information see
www.nonsuch-publishing.com